THE BUDDHA

[HIS LIFE & TEACHINGS]

DONNA RASKIN

evergreen

FOR JAMES

EVERGREEN is an imprint of
TASCHEN GmbH

© 2006 TASCHEN GmbH
Hohenzollernring 53, D-50672 Köln
www.taschen.com

© 2005 Fair Winds Press
© Text 2005 Donna Raskin

Printed in China

ISBN 3-8228-4981-2

Contents

PART THREE

Buddhism in the World

Buddha: A Man, Not a God, Savior, or Prophet

"BELIEVE NOTHING, NO MATTER
WHERE YOU READ IT OR WHO
HAS SAID IT, UNLESS IT AGREES
WITH YOUR OWN REASON
AND YOUR OWN COMMON SENSE."

—Buddha

In approximately 528 BCE, a thirty-five-year-old man named Siddhartha Gautama sat meditating beneath a fig tree when, in a moment of Enlightenment, he understood that he had figured out the path to *nirvana*, or the end of the suffering that is inherent in life. Previously, Siddhartha had lived the life of a prince and the life of an ascetic, but neither of these lifestyles had brought him happiness or been fulfilling. Then, in a final quest to escape from life's painful reality, he had vowed to meditate until Enlightenment came to him.

Siddhartha didn't figure out the meaning of life. To him, it was obvious: He had been taught by his family and his society that the meaning of life was to cease *samsara*, or the cycle of birth, death, and rebirth that every living thing experienced. In becoming the Buddha, or The Enlightened One, Siddhartha realized that the path out of samsara was the Middle Path, a life that is not too extreme in either denial or decadence. This path became what we call Buddhism.

Although named after the Buddha, Buddhism, the religion, is not a way to worship him. Buddha is honored by Buddhists around the world, but they do not deify him. Instead, they consider Buddha to be one of the people who got it right—there were buddhas before him, there will be buddhas after him, and, some Buddhists believe, there is a buddha inside each of us.

This particular Buddha lived a life of contrasts: rich and poor, decadent and austere, sheltered and wise. These extremes of good fortune and destitution created questions and emotional struggles for him, so he went in search of answers and in doing so, lived his life so well and with so much thoughtfulness and goodness that he found the path to Enlightenment. Then he taught thousands of people how to live so that they could do the same. Buddha continues to serve as an example of how to live to millions of people around the world, more than 2,000 years after his birth.

But that was just in the life of Siddhartha Gautama. Buddhists believe that all living things, including the Buddha, have a long series of past lives and reincarnations. To many Buddhists, the stories of Buddha's other lives are as important as the biography of Siddhartha.

Today's Buddhism

Buddhists live life without concern over an unseen God who judges them and with the example of the Buddha as a man who lived well. Thus, Buddhists do not actually describe their religion as "faith" but rather as a "practice." Indeed, Buddha (and all Buddhist teachers after him) always insisted that Buddhists should never accept any piece of information from a teacher, guru, or lama as fact without first thinking it through themselves. They are advised to use their own experience and their own ability to understand reality to find their own path to Enlightenment. The trick to finding your path, according to Buddha, is to learn how to think clearly, rationally, and with insight. Once you can do that, you'll live well and achieve Enlightenment.

Buddha was born more than 2,500 years ago in the India/Nepalese border area and found Enlightenment in India. During and after his lifetime, Buddhism gradually spread throughout Asia to Tibet, Sri Lanka, and Indonesia, as well as to China, Mongolia, Korea, and Japan. Over the past two centuries, Buddhism has found larger and larger audiences in the West. In each country, Buddhism changes with and is changed by its students.

Today, Buddhists are in yoga studios and ashrams in the West, work for peace and justice in China and Tibet, and preach non-violence in Africa and the states of the former Soviet Union. In the latter part of the twentieth century, two of the most influential Buddhists of our time—The Dalai Lama and Aung San Suu Kyi—were awarded Nobel Peace Prizes.

The Buddha's life and the example he sets are particularly relevant for people of the twenty-first century for numerous reasons. First, many of us live in violent places and Buddhism promotes ahimsa, or non-violence. Second, even when we live in relatively safe parts of the world, the larger picture is out of balance—entire cultures overconsume while others have too little.

Third, many individuals live out-of-balance lives, just as Siddhartha Gautama did. We overindulge with food, drink, or drugs, and then we try to be abstemious to compensate for the indulgence. And despite the educational, financial, and social opportunities available to most of them, Westerners often struggle with feelings of emptiness and a lack of meaning in their lives. Most of us know intuitively that the solution isn't to give up on the world around us, so somehow we have to find a place within us—and in the world—that works, that feels right, and that seems relevant.

The Buddha struggled with these same issues, and his answers work for millions of people long after the occurrence of his *parinirvana*—the physical death of his body and the final passage of his spirit into nirvana.

PART ONE

The Buddha's Life

"THERE IS A BUDDHA IN EACH OF US."

—Thich Nhat Hanh

Siddhartha Gautama/
Buddha Timeline

Although Siddhartha Gautama's exact birthday isn't known, we do know for certain that he lived in the sixth to fifth century BCE in the area that today includes much of India and Nepal. The life of the historical Buddha is inseparable from the legend of Buddha, but all aspects of his biography are communicated as truth within the Buddhist *dharma* (teaching).

563 BCE — The Wondrous Birth

After having visions and vivid dreams filled with signs and symbols, Queen Mahamaya gives birth to a son in Lumbini, Nepal. His father is King Suddhodana, ruler of the Sakya tribe, and names him Siddhartha (One Who Obtains Success). Seers predict that Siddhartha will become either a monarch or a buddha. His mother dies seven days after the birth and so his Aunt Prajapati begins to raise him.

563–547 BCE — The Luxurious Childhood

Siddhartha spends his childhood in his father's palace in Kapilavastu, Southern Nepal. During a plowing ceremony in his early childhood, Siddhartha has his first spiritual experience, which seems to foreshadow his future Enlightenment. Siddhartha is trained in spiritual disciplines, becomes proficient in archery, and learns the fighting and logic skills of a warrior, including hand-to-hand combat. At sixteen, Siddhartha marries his cousin, Princess Yasodhara, by arrangement of his father.

547–533 BCE—The Isolated Life of Indulgence
Siddhartha spends thirteen more years in the royal court. His father shields him from all discomforts and problems, going so far as to build three palaces for him: one for the cold season, one for the hot season, and one for the rainy season. Despite this grand way of life, he senses that something of significance is missing.

533 BCE—The Four Sights
For the first time in his life, Siddhartha leaves the palace and has four significant sights: a decrepit old man, a person who is very ill, a corpse being cremated, and an ascetic. When these sights are explained, he learns about old age, sickness, and death which he's not known about before. He also learns about the Hindu society surrounding him and how little control people have over their station in life (the caste system).

533 BCE—The Renunciation
On the night of his twenty-ninth birthday, soon after his son is born, Siddhartha gives up his life as a prince and leaves his father's castle in secret. He becomes an ascetic in the hopes of escaping from the tragedy of life.

533–528 BCE—The Ascetic Life
Now a *bodhisattva* (future buddha), Siddhartha roams India as a penniless and homeless ascetic. He becomes a disciple of two famous Brahman teachers and later

joins five other ascetics in forming a small community. After a long and exhausting period of searching and self-mortification, Buddha is close to death from starvation. He becomes disillusioned with asceticism due to his weakness and illness, so he gives up that lifestyle to continue his search for truth through the practice of meditation.

528 BCE—Enlightenment
After being tempted by the symbolic daughters of Mara (i.e., a devilish deva, or spirit) while meditating under a Bodhi tree in Bodh-Gaya, India, Siddhartha, in one perfect moment, understands the way to salvation from suffering and achieves the Great Enlightenment. He spends seven weeks meditating under the Bodhi tree and becomes a buddha at the age of thirty-five.

528 BC—First Sermon
Buddha preaches to the five ascetics with whom he used to live and teaches them what he has learned. Upon hearing his talk, one of the disciples instantly attains the status of an *arahant* (one with Enlightened wisdom). All of the disciples become the first five members of the *sangha* (Buddhist community).

528–527 BC—Teaching
Buddha travels endlessly, explaining the dharma to thousands of people. Eventually, the converted begin to preach to the uninformed. The Buddha briefly returns to the palace of his father to convert most of his family.

523–483 BCE—Converting Larger Groups
In the forty-five years following his Enlightenment,
Buddha travels around Northern India to teach the
tenets of Buddhism. He is extremely successful and
attracts thousands of people who voluntarily decide
to follow his teachings. Buddha's success, however, does
not only attract admirers but also provokes envy. Thus,
some of his closest advisors plot to destroy him or kill
him. Still, overall, his popularity grows exponentially.

483 BCE—Release from Samsara
Now eighty, Buddha dies in a forest near Kusinagara,
Nepal, surrounded by many of his followers and his
servant Ananda. He passes into parinirvana, which
is both physical death and the passing into nirvana:
perfect happiness.

SIDDHARTHA THE PRINCE

The Birth
Around the year 563 BCE, an Indian queen named
Mahamaya dreamt of a white elephant entering and
passing through her body. This vision, which is the sign
of a buddha, showed her that although she had not been
declared physically pregnant, she would give birth.
Soon after, while traveling from her parents' home to
her husband's castle, the queen walked over to a tree
in Lumbini Park and, while standing and holding onto
a tree branch that had lowered itself from the sky,
painlessly bore a son. Some say she gave birth from
the side of her body, because the baby emerged clean,

smiling, and able to walk—and, as in later in his life, wherever he walked, lotus blossoms bloomed immediately and miraculously beneath his feet.

The queen and her husband, King Suddhodana, asked five wise men to name their son. They named him Siddhartha, which means "One Who Obtains Success." The seers declared that the boy would be either a buddha or a king. They said that if the prince saw someone old, sick, dead, or a monk, he would grow up to be a monk himself, rather than a powerful ruler, which is what the king wished for his son.

Then, seven days after she gave birth, Queen Mahamaya died. Her sister, Prajapati Gautama, raised Prince Siddhartha and the king vowed that the prince would never witness an unpleasant sight. The king made sure that Siddhartha would never see anyone old, sick, or unhappy, and that he was never told about death or poverty. He kept the boy within the confines of the palace walls and gave him a life infused with pleasure and luxury.

Despite his father's efforts to prevent him from becoming a monk, Siddhartha had one moment of foreshadowing when, during a celebration, he entered a deep, meditative trance without any warning or study. One other strange moment occured when, it was said, he won an archery competition against trained shooters despite his lack of instruction.

Siddhartha grew up to be a fortunate man: good-looking, strong, and intelligent. His father arranged for him to marry a cousin, Princess Yasodhara, when they were both sixteen, and he built them a sumptuous palace filled with entertainers and anything else they needed to be distracted from more earthly cares. Indeed, only healthy young people were allowed to enter Siddhartha's home.

Even in this life of uncomplicated luxury and pleasantries, however, Siddhartha always felt that something was missing or not quite right. He is said to have wondered aloud about his dissatisfaction, but those around him never mentioned the dark side of life that his father kept from him.

The Four Sights

Siddhartha eventually decided that it was time to see what was beyond the palace walls. He began to take short trips into the real world. On his first visit to a place not controlled by his father, Siddhartha traveled with Channa, his attendant and best friend. On this trip, he saw a white-haired, haggard, poor old man—like no one he had ever seen before. This person's obvious hardship stunned him. He was so confused about what he was seeing that he asked Channa to explain who the man was and what was wrong with him.

Channa explained, "This is an old man. Everyone gets old. And he is poor. Not everyone has as much money and comfort as you have, Siddhartha." Imagine hearing this for the first time at twenty-nine!

The sight and Channa's words disturbed Siddhartha, but they also aroused his curiosity. He felt compelled to go out again, realizing that this was part of what had kept him unsatisfied for all of these years —it was a clue to what was missing.

The next time Siddhartha left the palace, he saw and heard a person on the ground, writhing in agony. Once again, he asked Channa what was wrong, and this time Channa told him about sickness.

On his third trip out into the world, Siddhartha saw a body being carried to its cremation, so Channa explained death. Channa explained to Siddhartha that people in the outside world lacked control over their lives. Until then, Siddhartha had never realized how changeable life was, as his world inside the castle never altered and was always pleasant.

Indeed, he had had no idea that illness, hard work, grief, sadness, aging, pain, or anything negative even existed in the world—the world he had seen until this point had been made beautiful and perfect. Thus, the public sights of India and Nepal in that day and age— intense poverty, cremation, and unquestioned belief in karma and caste—must have shocked Siddhartha very much.

Finally, on his fourth trip beyond the castle walls, Siddhartha saw a man in yellow robes. Unlike the men he had previously seen, this man looked calm and peaceful. Channa then told Siddhartha about asceticism and a monk's (or ascetic's) life. The monk, Channa explained, had left a life of family and pleasure to instead find meaning and a way out of suffering. This idea inspired Siddhartha, so he decided to become a

monk to find a way out of the seemingly uncontrollable
cycle of aging, sickness, and death.

Meanwhile, Siddhartha's wife had just given birth to
a son, Rahula, and Siddhartha felt torn between the two
ways of life. He had lost all interest in the luxuries and
decadences his father had offered him, but now he had
responsibilities and attachments. Nevertheless,
Siddhartha decided that he must leave home and lead
the life of a monk in order to understand what causes
the suffering in life. So, while his wife and son slept, he
kissed them goodbye and left the palace.

LEAVING LUXURY FOR ASCETICISM

The Life of a Monk
Now twenty-nine years old, Siddhartha began to live
the life of a monk—he begged for his one meal of the
day, walked miles every day, and wore a yellow robe. In
those days, this was a common way for monks to live.
These men (women were not allowed to be monks)
believed that the key to releasing their souls from the
cycle of life and death was great suffering, so they ate as
little as possible, practiced extreme denial, and forced
their physical bodies to withstand enormous tests of
stress and pain, such as standing on one foot or sleeping
on boards of nails.

Bodhisattvas
At this time in India, being a mendicant monk who
begged for food wasn't seen as shameful. In fact, it was

just the opposite: Homelessness and begging were seen as spiritual lifestyles. In this non-capitalist society, wealthy men and royalty were privileged to honor those on religious quests by offering them food and shelter. Kings became both patrons and disciples to monks, nuns, and the men who chose to seek nirvana by detaching themselves from worldly life.

In addition to monks, there were *boddhisattvas*, or men and women who were destined not just to achieve Enlightenment for their own sake but also to help all people do so. Siddhartha would become one of these.

He went to study with two renowned Brahmans, seeking understanding about why suffering is part of life. His first teacher, Arada Kalama, taught him how to quiet his mind and meditate with focus and intention. Siddhartha grew so proficient at doing this that his teacher asked him to teach meditation, but Siddhartha found that this type of meditation alone could not bring him to a point of reaching Enlightenment, so he sought another mentor.

His second teacher, Udraka Ramaputra, taught him a type of meditation in which he was so relaxed that he was neither conscious nor unconscious. But this too, seemed to bring him serenity and not Enlightenment. Siddhartha grew discouraged by the answers these teachers offered and their apparent inability to understand them. He decided that he would be better off finding the answers to his own questions.

In his next attempt at Enlightenment, Siddhartha joined a group of five other ascetics, believing that great suffering would bring him closer to Enlightenment. For six years, he ate one grain of rice a day and meditated for many days in a row. Then, one day, he fainted, and a shepherd saw the unconscious Siddhartha and fed him some goat's milk and honey.

Upon waking, Siddhartha realized that without the shepherd's help, he would have died before attaining Enlightenment. Therefore, Siddhartha reasoned, the life of an ascetic was not the secret to the soul's release. He began to eat and live normally, and he left his former group of monks. But he was still on a quest.

Forty-Nine Days

After his health and his spirit returned, Siddhartha decided to meditate under a nearby tree until the answers came to him. As he meditated, he asked himself the following questions: "How does suffering begin? Can we free ourselves from it?"

As he began to release himself from any distracting images and thoughts, he became unaware of his physical surroundings. Siddhartha found that memories of his previous lives began to flood into his consciousness. He saw that good deeds and positive actions led to happiness and calm feelings and that bad actions created bad feelings and suffering. The origin of suffering, he determined, was in a person's belief that he and his needs were more important than the natural rhythm of life and than other people.

Before Siddhartha could pass into nirvana, he had to prove that he could act according to the laws of karma. Thus, he was tempted by Mara, a *deva* (spirit) who attempted to lure him away from the great peace of Enlightenment. Mara sent his three daughters, "Blissful to Behold," "Pleasurable to Others," and "Lust," to destroy the bodhisattva by revealing their bodies and assuming various poses. But the mind of the bodhisattva did not move for even a moment.

Then the three girls transformed themselves into five hundred beautiful girls, each of whom assumed an incalculable number of unusual poses designed to entice Siddhartha. But his strength of mind and spirit were so strong that he could only see the girls' evil spirits—which he then turned into flowers, transforming their unwholesome spirits into goodness.

In his final attempt to prevent Siddhartha's Enlightenment, Mara claimed that he himself was destined to be the Buddha because of his own previous good deeds. But then Siddhartha touched the earth and asked it to remember his own previous lives. The ground shook and Mara fled. Siddhartha suddenly was able to remember his own lives and to see past the lives of all others.

Then the universe shuddered, and at this moment, Buddha's spirit was released from its own questions and suffering: He attained *nirvana* or freedom from samsara. Thus, at age thirty-five, Siddhartha became the Buddha, or The Enlightened One.

ENLIGHTENMENT

The word "Buddha" denotes not just a single religious teacher who lived in a particular era but a type of person, of which there have been many over the years. (As an analogy, the term "American President" refers not just to one person but to everyone who has ever held the office of the American presidency.) The buddha Siddhartha Gautama, then, is simply one member in the spiritual lineage of buddhas, which stretches back into ancient history and forward into the future. A Buddha is any human being who has fully awakened to the true nature of existence, whose insight has totally transformed him or her beyond birth, death, and subsequent rebirth, and who is enabled to help others achieve the same Enlightenment.

The buddha Siddhartha did not claim any divine status for himself, nor did he assert that he was inspired by a god or gods. He did not claim to be a personal savior, but rather a teacher to guide those who chose to listen.

This guidance was called the Buddhadharma, or simply the dharma, which means, "law, doctrine, or truth." It says that anyone can attain what Siddhartha attained, regardless of age, gender, or caste.

Indeed, Buddhists believe there have been many buddhas who achieved Enlightenment on their own but who did not go on to teach others. Indeed, other buddhas have despaired of humans' limited capacity for understanding and so did not teach what they had learned. In fact, according to one story, the Buddha was afraid of this too, but the Vedic (early Hindu) god Indra interceded and requested that he teach despite his uncertainty.

It is what happened next that turned this new buddha into the Buddha: He decided that although he did not live in a world in which most people would understand his teachings, there would nevertheless be a few who would comprehend it. He decided to teach the dharma. This is what makes him the Buddha.

BUDDHA AS TEACHER

Buddha thought that perhaps his old friends the monks would be open to his teaching, so he went to see them. But because Buddha was now well fed and non-ascetic, his old friends believed that he had given up on his search for Enlightenment. They refused to see him, and even ignored him as he approached. But the closer he came, the more clearly they saw that he now had a white light around him, which signaled his state of nirvana. Thus, they offered him a seat and asked him to tell them his story. So begins the Buddha's first teaching of The Four Noble Truths (see p. 49).

One by one, these monks attained Enlightenment by following the Buddha's teachings. Soon, a wealthy young boy came to study with him, and then other young men from high-caste families left their homes to join the Buddha's sangha. Ultimately, he had sixty monks as students, and he asked them to leave the community and begin to teach others about the dharma. Buddha returned to Uruvela, teaching on his journey, and as time went on, more than 1,000 men became fully Enlightened.

Buddha then went to the king, Bimbisara, and taught him the dharma. King Bimbisara began to practice the Buddha's teaching and donated his Veluvana Park to the Buddha. It became the first Buddhist monastery.

As was the common practice among monks of all kinds, Buddha was still begging for food, so while he traveled the countryside teaching, Brahmins would feed him and offer him shelter. He would teach their children, many of whom would immediately become arahants.

At some point after his followers began traveling around India to teach the dharma, Buddha decided it was time to bring them all together. He held a conference at Veluvana, and 1250 monks, all fully Enlightened arahants, attended. The Buddha taught them that the essence of his belief was this: **Hurt no living thing, do good deeds, and purify your mind through clear thinking and meditation.**

Buddha Returns to His Family
When King Suddhodana invited his son to return to Kapilavatthu, Buddha came with his many disciples. They stayed outside of the city to continue begging for food, which irritated Buddha's father. The king went to see Buddha and yelled about him disgracing the family.

Buddha explained that he intended to follow the custom of the past buddhas, not to follow his ancestors.

He explained the dharma to his father, who, in turn, offered the Buddha and his followers food at the castle. After a delicious meal, the Buddha taught the dharma to everyone in the castle. Then he went to see his wife and son, who he hadn't seen in many years. His wife was very sad, but Buddha was able to tell her that she was in good standing because of karma.

Buddha's son, Rahula, was seven years old at the time, and the Buddha made him a first novice—that is, someone training to be a monk (or, possibly a nun). Buddha also began training his cousins, stepbrothers, and other princes in his clan, the Sakyas.

After King Suddhodana died, the Buddha's aunt, Lady Prajapati Gautama, decided to become a nun. The Buddha refused her, however, because she was a woman. She then went to Buddha's cousin Ananda, who also pleaded with Buddha to allow her to become a nun, but once again, the Buddha refused. Finally, the Buddha said it would be okay as long as the nuns followed the eight monastic rules. Thus, Prajapati Gautama became the first Buddhist nun. Ananda, Buddha's closest disciple, became Buddha's assistant.

Buddha's Enemies

The Buddha's existence continued to be connected to the everyday world of real people; thus, he was not loved by everyone, and he and his followers suffered through the jealousies and problems brought on by those who didn't understand or want to accept the dharma. Some of these issues came from within the sangha.

One jealous and vindictive person was Devadatta, another of Buddha's cousins. Because of his feelings, Devadatta left the sangha and befriended Prince Ajatsattu, son of King Bimbisara, one of the Buddha's most loyal followers. Devadatta encouraged the prince to kill his father so that he could become king. Prince Ajatasattu then starved his father to death and made Devadatta one of his advisers.

Because Devadatta felt more powerful than before, he decided that he would be able to kill the Buddha. First he tried to roll a large boulder onto Buddha, but the rock broke into very little pieces once it came close to him and only one sharp piece stabbed him in the foot.

Devadatta decided to try again. As the Buddha went around for alms one morning, Devadatta let a wild elephant loose. As the animal ran closer to Buddha, however, it became docile, due to the Buddha's kind nature.

Devadatta finally realized that he wouldn't be able to kill the Buddha. He did, however, feel that he would still be able to break up the Buddhist community. To do so, Devadatta decided he would have to be crafty. He asked the Buddha to make the rules for monks stricter and more difficult to adhere to. The Buddha, with this divine eye, understood Devadatta's intentions, so, in front of the sangha, Buddha said, "The monks can do as they wish on their specific paths. If you try to break up the sangha, Devadatta, you will reap the evil fruits of your intentions."

Still Devadatta was not deterred, so he invited some monks from the sangha to join him and he started a new community. One of the Buddha's true disciples entered the new community and explained to the monks their mistake and its potential consequences. The monks left Devadatta, and he became ill with the realization of the end results. Finally, he decided to return to the Buddha and change his ways, but he died on the way there.

Later Life

The Buddha taught the dharma for forty-five years, traveling all over the Ganges Plain of central India, always on foot. He stayed at monasteries and at people's homes. His daily life was usually the same: He rose before sunrise, bathed, and meditated, mostly to determine whom he might teach that day. Then he would beg for food, sometimes alone, and sometimes with his monks. He would teach, and he would take walks. At night, he would return to the monastery and give a dharma talk, and sometimes individual instruction, to the nuns and monks. He used the dharma to help solve people's practical problems, not just to enlighten them.

At the age of eighty, the Buddha was still mentally competent, but he felt his body getting weaker. He realized that he would die soon, so he decided to travel north to the Himalayas, where he was born. Without reaching home, he decided to spend the rainy season in Patali. There he became very ill.

He felt that he could die at peace because there were enough disciples, monks, and nuns to continue practicing and teaching the dharma. The sangha (community) was complete. He felt that at this time the dharma would be a better teacher than he personally would be. He foresaw, upon meditating, that he would die three months from that day, and he told Ananda so.

Before he could go peacefully, Buddha spoke to Ananda and his sangha. He told them to practice their meditation and good deeds not only for their own benefit, but also for the benefit of all others. He encouraged them, too, to teach the dharma to others.

The Buddha and Ananda traveled to places that had meant a lot to him during his travels. They went to Vesali and Pava, where they stopped in the garden of Cunda, and offered the dharma to Cunda and his family. Cunda took refuge in the dharma, but, unbeknownst to him (although Buddha knew), he served the Buddha a meal that would cause him to become ill.

Despite the Buddha's illness, he and Ananda continued on their journey and, on their way, they met a prince. The prince accepted The Three Jewels (see p. 49) and, in response, gave the Buddha two rolls of gold cloth. Buddha kept one and gave the other to Ananda.

Finally, the Buddha determined that it was time to rest. He asked Ananda to make a comfortable spot for him between two trees near Kusinara. He lay down on his right side but did not sleep. His body was ill, but his mind was at peace.

Ananda was distraught at the thought of losing the Buddha. He was sad not only because of the loss of his teacher but also because he had not yet become an arahant (i.e., Enlightened One) as many of his comrades had. Buddha sensed Ananda's fear and praised him in front of the other monks, saying that although Ananda had not become Enlightened, he was significant and valuable and of great importance to both the Buddha and the sangha.

Ananda then asked the Buddha if he would move to a more worthy place for his death, but the Buddha said no, that previously this spot had been prosperous and royal. Nevertheless, the Buddha instructed Ananda to go bring the nearby kings to come to him so that his body could be handled properly after his death.

Many people came to see the Buddha as he lay dying. One was Subhadda, a young man who had many questions about the sangha and the dharma. He felt that only the Buddha could help him. He asked Ananda again and again to allow him to see the Buddha before his death, and he finally did. He answered Subhadda's questions and, as asked, the Buddha ordained him as a monk. Subhadda was the last person to be ordained by the Buddha.

Buddha reminded the members of his sangha that all things change and nothing is permanent. The Buddha then began to meditate, more and more deeply, until his mind was pure, balanced, and focused.

Thus, the Buddha passed into parinirvana: the physical death of one life.

The Society and Religious World Around Siddhartha

From its mythical aspects to its acceptance of reincarnation, some aspects of the Buddha's story may not ring true to the modern ear. It's important, then, to understand the world that Siddhartha Gautama was born into. Indian society of the pre-Common Era was a world of wealth and education surrounded by a larger society of intense poverty. That world was spiritual, and the beliefs he had been taught infused the religion that became Buddhism.

CASTE

Buddha was born into a time when social classes weren't considered merely to be luck of the draw in terms of birth and representation of business skills. Instead, the class (or caste) you were born into—and stuck in through life—was considered a result of past-life karma. In other words, how wealthy or good looking or fortunate you were at birth was not just a social dictum but also a matter of religion. Thus, you couldn't earn or learn your way out of a caste. Society concluded and supported the idea that if you were born at a certain level, then there must be a reason, and you would stay there through your lifetime. However, you could change castes after your death from this life. Because, according to this thinking (which, by the way, was supported by main religions of the time, Hinduism and Jainism), your soul would transmigrate in the next lifetime.

The castes were Brahmins (priests), Kshatriyas (warriors or kings), Vaishyas (merchants), Shudras (servants), and, eventually, the Untouchables. It was against this caste system that many Buddhists adopted their views of reincarnation. They believed that good deeds, not the caste in which you were born, could help to alter your spiritual path.

PRINCIPLES OF HINDUISM

Buddha accepted the idea of karma as fact, so he created a philosophy based on the idea that suffering in life was punishment for bad deeds committed in a previous life. This concept is called samsara, or the cycle of birth, death, and rebirth. In this concept, our soul travels through time and we all repeat this cycle endlessly. What we are born as—insect, brahmin, slave— depends on our actions in the previous life.

In Hinduism and in the world Buddha was born into, the goal wasn't to be born royalty or a higher caste but to release your soul from its body and the samsara cycle in order to reunite your soul (atman) to the Brahman soul. Brahman was considered an unseen spirit that created the world and infused its spirit into all things. Its interior soul, atman, went into everyone's soul.

What draws one human soul to the universal soul was called yoga (or yoke). The final release of a soul is moksha. Practicing yoga—meditation and physical exercise—allowed you to experience the reality of nirvana and, at the same time, build up karma.

Buddhists and Hindus share the belief of karma and samsara. The difference between the two religions, at least in terms of karma and samsara, is that Hindus believe the soul is fixed, while Buddha postulated that people had the ability to change their soul and, thus, could get closer to Enlightenment and release themselves from the cycle of samsara.

This is where the Buddhist concept of anatman or non-self comes in. If we don't have a solid soul or self within our bodies in this life, then what is our soul or our self? Buddha believed that each person was a process: a person is always "becoming." Nevertheless, each person had five elements, one of which was the physical body.

The idea of transmigration—your soul moving to another body/being after your physical death—was a given in this society. Almost everyone believed in reincarnation and considered karma a fact of life. The symbol of this thinking was "the wheel of life." When one revolution of the wheel was complete, life began again with rebirth.

KARMA IN THE PRE-BUDDHISM WORLD
The concept of rebirth is unfamiliar to many Westerners. Its philosophical and traditional foundation was in India, where the theory of transmigration of souls

had existed long before it was written in the Upanishads around 300 BC.

The Sanskrit word karma literally means "action." The word refers to speech, deeds, and intentions, as well as the results of these actions. The idea of karma existed long before the time of Siddhartha, and he accepted its reality so completely that it became an important element of Buddhism.

Hindus believe that the soul is unchanging throughout all lives and has an ultimate identity. That soul, according to the Hindus, will reach nirvana in the same state it was in throughout its various lifetimes, no matter what physical form it took.

The problem with that philosophy, as Buddha saw it, was that people couldn't get out of their life situations to change their karma. That is, if you were born of a lowly cast, it was difficult to live a "good" life. You could live a "moral" life, but you couldn't accumulate what the upper castes said you needed in order to be born into a higher caste in your next life. Intention didn't matter; neither did goodness. For example, actions that were considered "evil deeds" during Buddha's time included passing between a Brahmin and the sunlight, thus creating a shadow on him.

Buddha replaced these social laws with a spiritual system based on your intention and how you lived your life. Following the Four Noble Truths surpassed the social laws of the time and enabled anyone to achieve Enlightenment. In Buddha's philosophy, suffering was not caused by being born into the wrong caste or by breaking a rule but rather was caused by your mindset and beliefs.

To be more specific, people are not responsible for their situation in life (i.e., being poor or being of a lower social class) but instead have to take responsibility for and improve their states of mind and the quality of their actions and speech if they are to live true Buddhist lives.

Jataka

Because reincarnation was considered a fact of life, Buddha was believed to have lived many lives before his birth as Siddhartha Gautama. The stories of his other lives are called jataka, or "birth" tales.

There are about 550 such tales. In some of them, he is an animal; in some, a human. In most of the stories, the hero (it's never a heroine, even when it's an animal) lives in or near Benares (now called Varanasi), a city in north central India on the Ganges River, the most sacred place for Hindus. Both Buddhists and Muslims have important religious sites nearby as well. Indeed, Buddhist history says that the newly Enlightened Buddha began his teaching in nearby Sarnath.

The Jataka Tales were published in Sri Lanka and then communicated through various countries for Buddhists around the world. They serve not just as tales about the Buddha's previous lives but also function as parables. To read them is to learn more about how to live in order to become released from samsara. Some Buddhists claim that these stories served as inspiration for Aesop and other parable writers.

Some jataka stories include *The Goat Who Saved the Priest* (which teaches wisdom), *Big Red, Little Red,* and *No-Squeal* (which attempts to explain what is wrong with jealousy), and *The Birth of a Banyan Tree* (to teach respect for elders). One, called *The Mosquito and the Carpenter*, is as follows:

Once upon a time, when Brahmadatta reigned in Benares, the bodhisattva worked as a trader. Near his place of business, there were many carpenters at work. One day, one of the men, who was bald, was working hard planing away at some wood. His head glistened like a copper bowl, and a mosquito settled on his scalp and stung him like a dart.

The carpenter said to his son, "My son, a mosquito is stinging me on the head. Drive it away."

"Hold still father," said the boy. "One blow will settle it."

Meanwhile, the bodhisattva came over as the father asked his son once again to get rid of the mosquito. The son went behind the old man's back, raised a sharp ax to kill the mosquito, and, as he brought it down, cut his father's head in two. The old man fell dead on the spot.

Said the bodhisattva, "Better than such a friend is an enemy with sense, whom fear of men's vengeance will deter from killing a man." Then he recited these lines: "Sense-lacking friends are worse than foes with sense; Witness the son that sought the gnat to slay, but cleft, poor fool, his father's skull in two."

So saying, the bodhisattva rose up and departed, passing away and rising into a new life days afterwards. But the carpenter, his body was burned by his kinsfolk.

The point here is that the bodhisattva both was wise in the situation and, more so, sought to teach others the moral of the story, so he was rewarded in his next life. The carpenter and his son were not so fortunate.

THE CONCEPT OF BUDDHA IN OTHER RELIGIONS

Jainism was the other major religion in Siddhartha's time, which espoused the idea of asceticism. One of Jainism's main prophets, Mahavira, lived in an era close to the Buddha (599–527 BCE). Jain texts record dialogues between the Buddha's disciples and Mahavira; Buddhist texts record dialogues between Mahavira's disciples and the Buddha.

In fact, the Buddha's creation of the "Middle Way" was supported by the Buddhist monastic community as a response to the Jain criticism that the Buddhist *Bhikkhus* (or mendicants who begged for alms) were "soft" and not living the rigorous lives of true ascetics. The Middle Way distanced Buddhist from Jain tradition by providing an alternative to "extreme asceticism" (i.e., Jainism) on one hand and Buddha's own princely hedonism on the other, as well as from the Hindu caste system. Before his Enlightenment, Buddha is known to have taken part in fasts, penances, and austerities found in the Jain tradition (e.g., the penance by five fires and the consumption of food using only one's cupped hands).

To this day, many Buddhist teachings, principles and terms remain identical to Jain traditions, and most comparative religious scholars consider Buddhism in large measure, an offshoot of Jainism.

Meanwhile, some Hindus consider Siddhartha Gautama the ninth incarnation of Vishnu, and in its scripture, Hinduism has both pro-Buddhist and anti-Buddhist passages. Japanese Shintos believe that Buddha is the god Kami. Those of the Bahá'í faith consider him an independent manifestation of God. Some Muslims believe Siddhartha Gautama is Dhul-Kifl, a prophet mentioned in the Koran; and some Christians believe that Siddhartha inspired the story of Josophat, who was sanctified by the Roman Catholic Church as a saint.

PART TWO

Buddha's Teachings

❖

"[BUDDHISM] TELLS US THAT OUR DESTINY AND FINAL CAUSE IS A CONDITION, NIRVANA, THAT EXCEEDS ALL TELLING BUT IS COMPLETELY FULFILLING. CURRENTLY WE ARE SCREENED FROM THAT CONDITION BY IGNORANCE AND THE RESULTANT DEMANDINGNESS OF OUR FINITE SELVES. THE ART OF LIFE, THEREFORE, CONSISTS IN OVERCOMING THE FUNDAMENTAL HUMAN DISABILITY OF EGOISM."

—Huston Smith

Spoken Teachings

Because Buddha only communicated with his disciples orally, he never wrote down any of his teachings. This was not uncommon at the time he lived, when few people wrote anything down and no one wrote a lot. Thus, even his disciples didn't write down what he said when he was alive. All communication, even spiritual and holy words, was spoken. Because all of his teachings were spoken and not written, the Buddhist sutras, or discourses, begin "thus have I heard." The teachings also are very repetitive so that they are easy to remember.

So before studying the Buddha's teaching, it's important to know that most of the words we associate with Buddhism, such as karma and nirvana are Sanskrit, but this isn't the language that Buddha spoke. Researchers believe that Buddha spoke Magadhi, a dialect of Sanskrit, but as far as we know, it is now a dead language. Sanskrit too is no longer spoken, but it is still understood.

Buddha asked his followers to speak in whatever language would be understood by those they were speaking to, so no language is considered "Buddhist" (as Latin is Catholic or Hebrew is Jewish), although most of the first sutras were written in Sanskrit. Another important language in the history of Buddhism is Pali, which was an Indian dialect. The Pali Canon was produced in Sri Lanka a few hundred years after the

Buddha's death and was considered the definitive tractate of the Buddha's teachings for centuries. Eventually, of course, the Buddha's teachings were translated. Some of the earlier translations were Chinese.

Buddhists believed that the words they were reading or hearing were straight from the Buddha's mouth and, therefore, holy. On the flip side of this belief , however, were many other Buddhists who believe that words can in no way communicate the significant concepts of Buddhism. For this reason, scripture is not nearly as important in Buddhism as it is in many other religions (e.g., Christianity and Judaism). In fact, Zen Buddhism explicitly believes in non-verbal communication.

Most Buddhists continue to rely on the spoken words of their teachers, rather than written words of ancient sages, to gain insight into their journey.

BUDDHIST IDEAS OF KARMA

The Buddhist concept of karma is subtly and yet significantly different from the classical Indian understanding of it: It denies the existence of a self. In Buddhism, the idea of self is merely an illusion caused by delusional and sloppy thinking. It says that people attach meaning to their perceptions, consciousness, mind, and body and call it a "self." In reality, according to the Buddha, there is no abiding entity that could be identified as a self because the states of perception, consciousness, and mind constantly change and are relative (i.e., if one aspect of them changes, everything changes).

Soul is the immortal version of the self that supposedly survives physical death, but Buddhism postulates that when the body dies, all mental activities cease, including thoughts and awareness, this proves that there is no soul. And, in fact, science has proven that consciousness is a function of our nervous system, so it seems difficult to believe that the conscious self survives death. It seems that the idea of a soul is simply a creation of the ego. Therefore, Buddhists deny the reality of both self and soul.

In Buddhism, the word "self" simply provides a reference frame for the mind-body phenomenon of living and conscious beings. We usually identify it with our body and with the stream of consciousness induced by sense perceptions and thoughts. In reality, however, what we call the "self" is neither long lasting nor detached from the rest of the world, other beings, and the creations of our own mind. Buddhists call this the "neither self nor non-self."

The big karmic question then becomes, "What is reborn if not the self?"

At first, it might appear that there is a contradiction between the canon of rebirth and a belief in the non-self, but it is more a matter of quality than reality.

To understand this better, imagine that we are essences, like ripples on the water. The universe is the water, and it moves due to many energies—wind, anything that touches it, and changes in its foundation. In this analogy, the universe is in motion due to karmic forces, just as a ripple, wave, or billow is like a person: it is a temporary phenomenon; it is just water in motion.

Is the wave a person? The ripple? The water? Or is it all just one greater whole?

Like the up and down of the ocean's waves, living things and beings come into life, exist, and die. Karma is one of the forces that make it rise and fall. It is therefore obvious that we should not focus on the temporary phenomenon of the wave, but on the force that causes, forms, and drives it. Buddhists understand karma as a natural law. There is no higher instance, no judgment, no divine intervention, and no gods that steer man's destiny. There is only the law of karma itself, which works on a global time frame. Deeds yield consequences in the next second, hour, day, month, year, decade, or lifetime, or in another distant lifetime.

The Non-Self

Buddhists believe that all phenomena are constantly changing. There is no "soul" according to Buddhists. Instead, there is a "non-self," or *anatman*.

What, then, is a human being? According to Buddha, a person is made up of five *skandhas* (parts): the *rupa* (body), *vedana* (feelings), *samjna* (opinions, or perceptions of experience as positive, negative, or neutral), *samskaras* (moods), and *vijnana* (consciousness).

The body is made up of four elements: earth, water, air, and fire. Feelings occur when the body experiences the outside world. Opinions occur based on those experiences of the outside world. And, finally, we are conscious when our body and our mind contact other people and the world. This last skandha is a kind of awareness.

Each of these aspects of a human being are forever changing and always impermanent—our physical bodies age and alter, our feelings and perceptions change as the world around us changes, and our moods change sometimes without our knowing why.

The point Buddha was making in delineating these aspects of a person is the significance of impermanence: that we shouldn't attach to any one thing in our lives because every aspect of our lives—our bodies, the world around us, our comfort level in it, our level of knowledge and wisdom—is always changing.

A renowned Buddhism teacher once likened our idea of a human self to a rainbow: A rainbow doesn't really exist as itself. It's a combination of light, water, and air. Without those three things, the rainbow doesn't exist, but we identify the rainbow as a rainbow without differentiating its three elements.

The Buddha would say that as human beings, we tend to identify more significantly with one or more elements of ourselves, such as our sex, our age, our marital status, or our wealth. We think of ourselves as "a woman" or "a husband" or "a 42-year-old." Buddha taught that these identifying characteristics not only fail to truly describe us but also limit our perception of ourselves. Furthermore, our mind's connection to these characteristics limits our spiritual development.

Not having a "self" brings an interesting aspect to the question of karma, then: If there is no self, how can you be "rewarded' or "punished" over lifetimes on the path to Enlightenment? In Buddhism, it doesn't work that way. Instead, Buddha taught that karma isn't the deed itself but rather the intention—the mental conception of goodness and good wishes—that endures as positive energy in a soul's consciousness. This consciousness endures throughout one lifetime and into the next, although it isn't part of a body. It's a state of goodness that has energy.

Although karma actually means cause, it also means effect—that is, was the energy *punya* (good) or *papa* (bad)? All intentions and acts have karmic consequences, and the results of those consequences determine one's rebirth after death.

Rebirth: Levels of Being
You can know the rough worth of someone's karmic energy by his or her status at birth. But karma is not, ultimately, the only thing that matters, nor is it a measure of a person's fate or destiny. Indeed, when we are considering the status of a person at birth, we are missing some of the point of Buddhist thinking. People, no matter what their social class or position (or looks or wealth), are all considered to be the most positive state of being, of which there are six. Human birth—and its attendant opportunities for consciousness and awareness—is considered an opportunity. Buddha recognized, of course, that all people had different abilities and levels of fortune, but he also

believed that all human beings have the opportunity to become Enlightened.

First Realm

Human beings are conscious and can choose to act out of ignorance or craving, no matter what their station or position in life.

Second Realm

The second realm of being is a deva, and these deities live in heaven. The good news? You're in heaven—no job, no problems. The bad news? With no struggle comes no way of advancing your karma. Plus, you've got the worrisome attachment problem—it may seem like nirvana, but it's not. You want to leave in order to keep advancing.

That's why it's the second realm and not the first.

Third Realm

On the flip side, you could also be reborn as a demon, which is the third realm. You are motivated by anger and can work magic because of it. Many Buddhists believe that it is these demons that cause problems for humans.

Fourth Realm

The fourth realm of being houses pretas, or restless spirits. These are kind of like ghosts, subtle beings of energy that are working through their previous attachments to human beings. Some Buddhists recognize these spirits by leaving food and drink for them as they struggle to regain a physical body.

Fifth Realm

Beings in the fifth realm live in purgatory. There are many types of hell, according to the Buddhist, and most involve extreme discomfort, such as cold or heat, or real pain, such as torture. This realm is mostly reserved for human beings who have committed truly immoral acts, such as hurting others or stealing.

Sixth Realm

The sixth realm is the animal realm, and it is considered the worst because animals eat each other, have only their instincts, and have very little ability to commit positive karmic acts, although some animals can do good.

Nevertheless, Buddhists put a lot of energy into acts of karma (the good kind) because they believe the rewards are inherent in those acts.

Karmic Activity

There are four levels of karmic activity: *dana* (unselfish generosity), *shila* (being moral), *svarga* (heaven or positive rebirth), and *dharma-deshana* (teaching dharma or showing others the Four Noble Truths). Most Buddhists (i.e., not monks or nuns) practice dana.

The philosophy surrounding karma and rebirth went like this: A person's soul (atman) was considered part of the universe's "soul," and the smaller the atman became (through loss of ego) the higher its level of rebirths or reincarnations. Your soul became less ego-driven by living well; thus, your karma (act) made your ego smaller. In this way, you attained moksha, or salvation, and your soul dissolved into the Universe. The Buddha explain how Buddhists could do this in The Four Noble Truths and The Noble Eightfold Path. First, the importance of intention cannot be overlooked. Action, taught the Buddha, occurs only because of volition and is absolutely (and, in some ways, merely) a result of intention. Furthermore, intention only exists because of thought so thinking clearly, intelligently, and with wisdom is the first step toward Enlightenment.

That said, the quality of any action is often what the rest of the world sees—few of us can fully intuit a person's intention or thoughts. Therefore, the Buddha ultimately described actions with ethical terms. They are either good or bad, both good and bad, or indifferent.

The Buddha encouraged people to use their own intuition and intelligence to determine what actions have which ethical qualities, even though everyone's discernment is in relation to a person's state of mental development. A wise person with strong thinking skills and an open, intuitive mind can more easily clearly understand another's mental activities and actions in an ethical dimension; a deluded person will find it almost impossible to do so.

And this is true not just of figuring out others, but also of figuring out yourself.

Delusions
Delusions can occur because of three defilements: confused thinking, greed, and hatred. These problems

blur the view and increase the level of confusion in an individual or group.

In the end, Buddhists hold that the quality of a person's thinking, intentions, and actions affect, because of the retributive process of karma, more than one lifetime. Rebirth or reincarnation is often referred to as *walking the wheel of life*. It is the process of being born over and over again in different times and different situations, possibly for many thousands of times, and is entirely based upon the quality of previous lifetimes.

Accumulated Karma

Karma has another aspect: If delusion, greed, inappropriate passion, and aversion are present, we generate karma. Further, we eventually accumulate unmaterialized karma (that is, karma that hasn't been balanced) in this or in a past lifetime, so there will follow a next lifetime in which the accumulated karma will take form. Only when all accumulated karma is balanced (i.e., negative karma has been made good) and the generation of new karma is calmed can one enter the stream that leads to nirvana.

Once a person enters the stream that leads to nirvana, they no longer have to focus on creating positive karma. Although wholesome karma leads to entering the stream, it does not necessarily lead to nirvana; only the extinguishment of all karmic forces leads to nirvana.

THE THREE JEWELS

Buddha instructed his disciples to "take refuge" in The Three Jewels: the Buddha, the dharma, and the sangha. Buddha didn't mean the word "refuge" in the English sense of "hiding" or "escape." Rather, he meant a place of safety, like home is to most people. This idea, coupled with the meditation practice, has made some people think Buddhism is about hiding or avoiding reality; instead, it is just the opposite. Buddhists strive to face reality and see everything clearly and without ego.

Taking refuge is more than an abstract concept. Taking refuge actually means following in the footsteps of those who have previously sought Enlightenment. Truly committed Buddhists actually take part in a ceremony and perform the Triple Refuge Ritual, in which they recite three times, "To the Buddha I go for refuge, to the dharma I go for refuge, to the sangha I go for refuge" (see Becoming a Buddhist in Part Three). In a more general sense, refuge means turning toward Buddhism and its tenets in your life.

THE FOUR NOBLE TRUTHS

When the Buddha was awakened, one of the concepts he grasped was encapsulated in The Four Noble Truths, which are the four elements that explain why suffering exists in our lifetime:

Dukkha: Life is unsatisfactory, confused, and chaotic, and we all suffer, either from emotional stress or, equally, physical ailments. We all feel unhappy. The Noble Truth of suffering is this: birth is suffering; old age is suffering; sickness is suffering; death is suffering; sorrow and lamentation, pain, grief, and despair are suffering; association with the unpleasant is suffering; dissociation from the pleasant is suffering; not to get what one wants is suffering. In brief, the five aggregates (skandhas) of attachment are suffering.

Samudaya: There is a cause to our suffering. We suffer because we feel attachment to ideas, desires, wants, and needs. Each of those yearnings is rooted in ignorance or ego. The Noble Truth on the Origin of Suffering is this: it is in this thirst that produces re-existence and re-becoming, bound up with passionate greed. It finds fresh delight now here and now there, namely, the thirst for sense pleasures; thirst for existence and becoming; and thirst for non-existence.

Nirodha: There is an end to our suffering and that is nirvana.

Margha: The path that leads out of suffering is the Noble Eightfold Path.

In more detail:

First Noble Truth
Buddhists believe we cause our own pain and suffering because of the way we think and the way we perceive events in our lives. Human nature is imperfect, as is the world we live in. We all live through physical suffering, such as pain, sickness, injury, tiredness, old age, and,

eventually, death. We all endure psychological suffering, such as sadness, fear, frustration, disappointment, and depression.

Of course, there are different degrees of suffering. In addition, there are positive experiences in life that we perceive as the opposite of suffering, such as love, comfort, health, and happiness. Even with its goodness and sweetness, however, life is imperfect and incomplete because we have no control over our lives and we know we are going to die. And, along the way, everything can change: We are never able to keep goodness, happiness, and health.

Second Noble Truth

Human beings are attached to transient things, and the ignorance that causes this attachment causes our suffering. Transient things include the physical objects that we collect and consume, as well as our ideas and the self-concepts that feed our egos.

Ignorance is not fully understanding and accepting the ways our minds work. It is attaching ourselves to impermanent things. Some examples of suffering are lust and desire, inexplicable passion, materialism, the love of power, striving for fame and importance, and, more importantly, craving, or attaching your happiness to, needing, or wanting one or more than one of these things. None of them will ever bring about everlasting happiness. Their loss is inevitable, as is our boredom with them, which is why we always want more. Thus, suffering will always follow even the happiest of accomplishments and feelings. Objects of attachment also include the idea of a "self," which is a delusion, because we are merely a part of the ceaseless becoming of the universe.

In the biggest picture, of course, we have no release from this suffering because we all will die. None of us want to die, and, more than that, we are stuck in the cycle of being born and reborn into a life that brings us pain and only temporary moments of happiness over which we have no control.

Third Noble Truth

Suffering can be ended by detaching and letting go of craving. Nirvana extinguishes all forms of clinging and attachment. People can end their emotional suffering by removing their attachment to desires and their ideas of themselves. Attaining and perfecting detachment is a long process that ultimately results in nirvana. Nirvana means release from the struggles within the mind—worries, fears, complexes, self-delusions, and egotistical ideas. If you haven't compre-hended the Four Noble Truths and understood the concepts of Buddhism, then there is no way to achieve Enlighten-ment and reach nirvana.

Fourth Noble Truth

That's because there is a path to the end of suffering, explained by Buddha in The Noble Eightfold Path. It is a way of life defined by The Middle Path, living between the two extremes of excessive self-indulgence and excessive asceticism; it leads to the end of samsara.

Following The Noble Eightfold Path is specific and significant. It means not just wandering through life with Buddhism on your mind, but actually taking part in the specific actions detailed on the Path.

THE NOBLE EIGHTFOLD PATH

Instead of telling them to take his word that The Four Noble Truths were true, Buddha recommended that his disciples follow The Noble Eightfold Path to determine whether his whole plan actually worked for them.

Although some people perceive the Eightfold Path to be a series of steps, it's actually a holistic entity. A person practices each "step" simultaneously and focuses on all equally. The Path includes Right View, Right Intention, Right Speech, Right Action, Right Livelihood, Right Effort, Right Mindfulness, and Right Concentration.

The "steps" in the Eightfold Path can be divided into three categories: Wisdom (through understanding the reality of life and thinking clearly), Ethical Living (acting kindly, speaking kindly, and earning a clean and honest living), and Mental Development (having good, pure intentions, and practicing meditation to encourage living and thinking well).

All of the "steps" are interlinked: There is no way to practice one without the others. The Noble Eightfold Path is practical, not just spiritual. Indeed, Buddha and

Buddhists put great emphasis on its usefulness. Through its practice, a person can live at a higher (or deeper) level of spirituality and ultimately reach nirvana.

The Eightfold Path is like a Moebius strip—it has no beginning and no end, but must be conceived of and practiced.

Wisdom

1. Right View
When practicing Right View, a person sees and understands the difference between reality and delusions, as well as the self and the non-self. To that person, everything is clear. Furthermore, with the ability to see clearly, he or she is able to grasp entirely the Four Noble Truths.

At the same time, Right View defines the intellectual and cognitive aspect of wisdom. It means seeing things truthfully and honestly, grasping the reality of impermanence, and understanding the reasons that desire and attachment make life more difficult and less fruitful. When practicing Right View, people easily understand the laws of samsara and karma. Right view is not just a matter of intelligence because it also concerns wisdom, which is more than being smart. It's more than just thinking about issues: It's about being able to use and understand the concepts that the Buddha taught. It begins with the acceptance and the insight of the First Noble Truth (i.e., that we are all subject to suffering) and ends with understanding of the Other Three Truths (that we can release ourselves from this suffering and achieve nirvana). Because our view of the world, or our mind's paradigm, creates our thoughts and, therefore, our actions, Right View allows for the possibility of all of the next steps of the Eightfold Path.

2. Right Intention

Right Intention refers not to what we do but to why we do it and how we do it—our meaning and our plan. Right Intention is best described as a personal commitment to morality, ethics, and clear thinking without attachment or delusions. The Buddha further defined the three types of Right Intention:

1. Renunciation or rejection of attachment and craving

2. Good will, meaning the intention to be positive and restrain oneself from anger, hatred, negativity, envy, greed, and other rejecting feelings and actions

3. Ahimsa, or harmlessness, meaning not to hurt any living thing, either through violence, physical actions, or hurtful words or deeds

Ethical Living

3. Right Speech

Right speech concludes the three principles of ethical conduct in the Eightfold Path. Ethical conduct is part of a moral discipline. Speech is important in Buddhism because words are as powerful as actions and, in fact, are no different to the Buddha. Buddha explained right speech this way: abstaining from false speech, especially from telling deliberate lies and from speaking deceitfully; abstaining from slanderous speech and from using words maliciously against others; abstaining from harsh words that offend or hurt others; and abstaining from idle chatter that lacks purpose or depth (i.e., gossip). Everyone should tell the truth; speak kindly, gently, and lovingly; and talk only when necessary.

4. Right Action

The second ethical principle, Right Action, refers to deeds, which include behaviors and the way we treat others. The Buddha explained it like this: To abstain from harming, especially to abstain from taking life (including suicide), and from doing harm intentionally or delinquently; to abstain from taking what is not given, which includes stealing, robbery, fraud, deceitfulness, and dishonesty; and to abstain from sexual misconduct. Positively formulated, Right Action means to act kindly and compassionately, to be honest, to respect the belongings of others, and to keep sexual relationships harmless to others.

5. Right Livelihood

Right Livelihood means that one should earn one's living in a righteous way and that wealth should be gained legally and peacefully. The Buddha mentions four specific activities that harm other beings and that one should avoid:

1. Selling, buying or trading in weapons

2. Dealing in living beings (including raising animals for slaughter as well as slave trade and prostitution)

3. Working in meat production and butchery

4. Selling intoxicants and poisons, such as alcohol and drugs

Furthermore, a person should avoid any other occupation that would violate the principles of Right Speech and Right Action.

Mental Development

6. Right Effort

Although Right Effort is the sixth step on the path, it is, at the same time, a prerequisite for the other principles of the path, because without effort—which really means how we try —nothing can be achieved. Misguided effort distracts the mind from its task, and confusion will be the consequence. In other words, if you put effort into achieving something that isn't worthy or significant, then you are distracting yourself from the path.

Mental energy is the force behind Right Effort; it can occur in either wholesome or unwholesome states. The same type of energy that fuels desire, envy, aggression, and violence can also fuel self-discipline, honesty, benevolence, and kindness. Right Effort is detailed in four types of endeavors, which rank in ascending order of perfection:

1. To prevent the arising of unarisen unwhole some states

2. To abandon unwholesome states that have already arisen

3. To arouse wholesome states that have not yet arisen

4. To maintain and perfect wholesome states already arisen

7. Right Mindfulness

Right Mindfulness is the controlled and perfected faculty of cognition. It is the mental ability to see things as they are, with clear consciousness. Usually, the cognitive process begins with an impression induced by perception, or by a thought. It does not, however, usually stay with the mere impression. Instead, we almost always conceptualize sense impressions and thoughts immediately. We interpret them in relation to other thoughts and experiences, which naturally go beyond the actuality of the original impression. The mind then posits concepts, joins concepts into constructs, and weaves constructs into complex interpretative schemes. All of this happens only half consciously, and as a result, we often see things obscured.

Right Mindfulness is anchored in clear perception, and it penetrates impressions without getting carried away. It enables us to be aware of the process of conceptualization so that we actively observe and control the way our thoughts go. Buddha accounted for this process by describing the four foundations of mindfulness:

1. Contemplation of the body
2. Contemplation of feeling (repulsive, attractive, or neutral)
3. Contemplation of the state of mind
4. Contemplation of phenomena

8. Right Concentration

The eighth principle of the path, Right Concentration, refers to the development of a mental force—namely, concentration—that occurs in natural consciousness, although at a relatively low level of intensity. In this context, concentration is described as one-pointedness of mind, meaning a state in which all mental faculties are unified and directed onto one particular object. Right Concentration for the purpose of the eightfold path means wholesome concentration (i.e., concentration on wholesome thoughts and actions).

The Buddhist method of choice to develop Right Concentration is through the practice of meditation. The meditating mind focuses on a selected object. It directs itself onto it, sustains concentration, and intensifies concentration, step by step. Through this practice, it becomes natural to apply elevated levels of concentration in everyday situations.

THE FIVE PRECEPTS

The Five Precepts are a shortened version of a moral

code that all Buddhists, whether monks or lay people, can undertake. They are as follows:

> I undertake the precept to refrain from harming living creatures.
>
> I undertake the precept to refrain from taking that which is not freely given.
>
> I undertake the precept to refrain from sexual misconduct.
>
> I undertake the precept to refrain from incorrect speech.
>
> I undertake the precept to refrain from intoxicants that lead to loss of mindfulness.

Some of these precepts seem clear, such as "refrain from harming living creatures," meaning that you shouldn't kill (which goes along with the concept of ahimsa). Likewise, "refrain from taking that which is not freely given" prohibits stealing.

Other precepts, however, are less clear. "Refraining from sexual misconduct," for example, can be open to interpretation. For a monk, it could mean everything from not having sexual thoughts to celibacy. For a layperson, however, refraining from sexual misconduct might mean remaining faithful to a spouse or not using sexuality for material gains.

Meanwhile, refraining from intoxicants can mean everything from not drinking alcohol to not smoking cigarettes. In general, however, incorrect speech means refraining from slander, gossip, insults, and hurting with words.

In some schools of Buddhism, committed lay people or aspiring monks take an additional three to five ethical precepts on holy days. They might, for example, refrain from eating after noon, or they may fast for a day. The precepts are a condensed form of Buddhist ethical practice. They are often compared with the Ten Commandments of Judaism and Christianity, but the precepts are different in two respects: First, they are to be taken as recommendations, not commandments. This means the individual is encouraged to use his or her own intelligence to apply these rules in the best possible way. Second, it is the spirit of the precepts—not the text of them—that counts. Thus, the guidelines for ethical conduct must be seen in the larger context of the Eightfold Path.

The number of precepts that Buddhists undertake can vary. The first five precepts are mandatory for every Buddhist, although the fifth precept is often not observed because it bans the consumption of alcohol. Precepts six through ten are laid out for those in preparation for monastic life and for devoted lay people unattached to families. When eight precepts are followed, numbers eight and nine are combined and the tenth is omitted. Lay people may observe the eight precepts on Buddhist festival days. Ordained Theravada monks, however, undertake no less than 227 precepts, which include abstaining from such things as:

- taking untimely meals
- dancing, singing, music and watching grotesque mime

- use of garlands, perfumes and personal adornment
- use of high seats
- accepting gold or silver

The phrasing of the precepts is very concise and, yet, at the same time, leaves much open to interpretation. What are untimely meals? Does a glass of wine cause heedlessness? Once again, clear thinking and following the Eightfold Path is supposed to help monks and nuns figure out the answers for themselves.

THE THREE MARKS
OF CONDITIONED EXISTENCE

The Buddha postulated the Four Noble Truths based on his idea that human existence had three characteristics or "marks."

The marks are like a triangle—each one is as significant as the other two. The first quality of existence is *anitya*: transience and impermanence. According to Buddha, all things are transient, impermanent, and illusory. Everything changes, including things we believe to be solid, such as rocks and trees and other physical forms. A modern person might align this concept with the idea of atoms and energy, but at the time of Buddha, these concepts did not exist. The Buddha did, however, realized that our perception of permanence was inherently false. Likewise, more importantly, all experiences are impermanent. Everything is made up of parts, and each thing depends on a certain combination of conditions for its existence. And because conditions are constantly changing, then all things are both constantly being born, changing, and dying. Nothing lasts. (See Buddhism and Modern Science in Part Three.)

The second mark is anatman, or the lack of a permanent soul. Hindu philosophy conceived of the self as an unchanging, permanent essence. This concept is related to the idea of Brahman, which was regarded as the ultimate atman for all beings. In other words, it had previously been believed and accepted that an unchanging essence would reap the benefits of karma and could thus one day reach Enlightenment. The Buddha, however, rejected the idea of atman and permanence. Instead, he insisted on changeability and impermanence, believing there was no unchanging essence within people or things, but rather that people were made of ever-changing qualities. Therefore, Buddha taught that preconceived notions of a substantial self were wrong and that people believed in a "self" because of ignorance and attachment.

Some people have misunderstood this idea of a non-self and equated it with a form of nihilism (i.e., a philosophy that rejects the moral and ethical values of our existence). However, Buddhism does not reject the concept of existence or of its value; instead, it questions our attachment to the concepts, ideals, and values that we use to prove the importance of our existence. Some would say, actually, that it is more closely related to the idea of Sartre's *Being and Nothingness* than to nihilism. Buddhism, therefore, has more in common with existentialism than with other Western philosophies.

The third mark of existence is dukkha (suffering). Dukkha occurs because of our ignorance and inability to understand the reality of the first two marks. We suffer because, as humans, we desire lasting happiness and peace of mind. But we look for this satisfaction within a world that is constantly changing. At the same time, even our perception of our self (i.e., our idea of what would make us happy) is deceptive. We perceive a "self" and act to please that "self" by making choices, but we are ultimately disappointed. However, we continue on this cycle by trying to find new and improved ways of making our "self" happy.

In order to develop *panna*, or insight and wisdom, it is not enough to understand these ideas intellectually. You have to truly make these concepts your reality.

MEDITATION

Meditation is a significant part of a Buddhist practice because it encourages and teaches insight, wisdom, and mindfulness. The Buddha's meditation practice was intense both before and after his Enlightenment. There are two types of meditation important to Buddhists: *vipassana* (insight) and *samatha* (calm abiding or, as it is sometimes translated, concentration).

During any type of meditation, the meditator strives to allow thoughts, fears, concerns, and worries to drift out of his consciousness, allowing for a sense of mindfulness. Mindfulness is the gift of openness and consciousness; it is an awareness of what's around you without a sense of judging or creation of an opinion. Mindfulness is a quality that meditators strive for not just in their meditation poses but in their daily lives. By practicing mindfulness during meditation, people are able to carry the skill into the rest of their lives.

People who meditate use a variety of tools to encourage mindfulness. First, they usually practice in quiet or with soothing music. Second, they focus on their breathing. Staying conscious of inhaling and exhaling takes their mind away from their thoughts and focuses their awareness onto something they can control. This consciousness of breath can soothe mind and spirit—as the breath slows, the mind relaxes.

Specific types of meditation use more tools. Vipassana meditation, for example, employs a consciousness of the breath and goes further by asking the meditator to focus on one element of his body or on something around him, such as a candle or a mantra. This focus allows the mind to float around that element of concentration so that the worries, thoughts, and concerns that usually fill the mind disappear.

Samatha meditation, on the other hand, only uses the breath, with no outside focus. This helps the mind to empty and go into a trance. Some Buddhists refer to this meditation as samadhi, or trance.

When a meditator rises from his seat, the feeling of peacefulness and serenity usually remains with him so that when something occurs (and remember, something is always occurring, as everything is always changing), the person is more able to remain open-minded and stay mindful or conscious (i.e., to respond without attachment).

VEGETARIANISM

The first precept in Buddhism advocates ahimsa, which most Buddhists believe to prohibit killing. For this reason, many Buddhists do not eat the meat of animals, although the Buddha actually made a distinction between killing an animal and eating meat, stressing that the food a person eats can't defile a person—only immoral conduct can.

During the Buddha's time, there was no general rule requiring monks to refrain from eating meat. In fact, at one point, the Buddha specifically refused to institute vegetarianism, and the Pali Canon records the Buddha himself eating meat on several occasions. Monks in ancient India were expected to receive all of their food by begging and to have little or no control over their diets.

However, there were rules prohibiting certain types of meat, such as human, leopard, or elephant meat. Monks were also prohibited from consuming meat if the monk witnessed the animal's death or knew that it was killed specifically for him. This rule was not applied to commercial purchase of meat in the case, for example, of a general who sent a servant to purchase meat specifically to feed the Buddha. Therefore, eating commercially purchased meat was not prohibited.

On the other hand, certain Buddhist sects (specifically the Mahayana sutras, or discourses) argue against eating meat. In those sutras, the Buddha says "the eating of meat extinguishes the seed of great compassion," adding that he prohibits all and every kind of meat and fish consumption, even of animals found already dead. Also in this sutra, the Buddha predicts that later monks will "hold spurious writings to be the authentic dharma," and will concoct their own sutras and mendaciously claim that the Buddha allows the eating of meat, whereas in fact (he says) he does not. Of course, this fighting over the veracity of various sutras is just one reason that there are numerous Buddhist schools).

Likewise, the Buddha comes out in favor of vegetarianism in the Lankavatara Sutra, saying that "the eating of the flesh of fellow sentient beings" is "incompatible with the compassion which a bodhisattva should strive to cultivate." Numerous other Mahayana sutras also prohibit the consumption of meat.

Today, different schools and cultures of Buddhism hold different beliefs toward vegetarianism. In Southeast Asia and Sri Lanka, Theravada monks are bound by their vinaya (i.e., sutras regarding monks) to accept almost any food that is offered to them, which is often meat. These monks accept alms as part of their commitment. Chinese and Vietnamese monks, however, eat no meat.

In Japan and Korea, monks practice vegetarianism when training at a monastery but eat meat at other times in their life. Buddhists in Tibet eat meat as a rule because vegetables are quite scarce. Their canonical texts, The Nikaya Sarvastivada, do not promote vegetarianism.

Lay Buddhists in the both the East and West generally do not follow any specific dietary guidelines.

THE FOURTEEN MINDFULNESS TRAININGS

Because many of today's Buddhists teachers recognize and accept that the language and habits of traditional Buddhism may strike today's students as off-putting, some of them have tried to update the language of the sutras, vows, and precepts. This is acceptable because, of course, all of the Buddhist writings are translations upon translations, so whatever words are chosen that are not in the Buddha's language are already approximations. Also, Buddhists strive to make their teaching useful and clear-thinking, so a bodhisattva living today must learn to speak the language of those whom he is trying to teach—or so the Buddha taught, even 2,500 years ago.

The following teaching comes from Thich Nhat Hanh (see Part Three), whose sangha, Plum Village, helps lay people of today embrace the precepts.

The First Mindfulness Training: Openness
Aware of the suffering created by fanaticism and intolerance, I am determined not to be idolatrous about or bound to any doctrine, theory, or ideology, even Buddhist ones. Buddhist teachings are guiding means to help me learn to look deeply and to develop my understanding and compassion. They are not doctrines to fight, kill, or die for.

The Second Mindfulness Training:
Non-attachment to Views
Aware of suffering created by attachment to views and
wrong perceptions, I am determined to avoid being
narrow-minded and bound to present views. I will learn
and practice non-attachment from views in order to be
open to others' insights and experiences. I am aware
that the knowledge I presently possess is not changeless,
absolute truth. Truth is found in life, and I will observe
life within and around me in every moment, ready to
learn throughout my life.

The Third Mindfulness Training:
Freedom of Thought
Aware of the suffering brought about when I impose
my views on others, I am committed not to force others,
even my children, by any means whatsoever—such
as authority, threat, money, propaganda, or indoctrina-
tion—to adopt my views. I will respect the right of
others to be different and to choose what to believe and
how to decide. I will, however, help others renounce
fanaticism and narrowness through compassionate
dialogue.

The Fourth Mindfulness Training:
Awareness of Suffering
Aware that looking deeply at the nature of suffering can
help me develop compassion and find ways out of
suffering, I am determined not to avoid or close my eyes
before suffering. I am committed to finding ways,

including personal contact, images, and sounds, to be with those who suffer, so I can understand their situation deeply and help them transform their suffering into compassion, peace, and joy.

The Fifth Mindfulness Training:
Simple, Healthy Living
Aware that true happiness is rooted in peace, solidity, freedom, and compassion, and not in wealth or fame, I am determined not to take as the aim of my life fame, profit, wealth, or sensual pleasure, nor to accumulate wealth while millions are hungry and dying. I am committed to living simply and sharing my time, energy and material resources with those in real need. I will practice mindful consuming, not using alcohol, drugs or any other products that bring toxins into my own and the collective body and consciousness.

The Sixth Mindfulness Training: Dealing with Anger
Aware that anger blocks communication and creates suffering, I am determined to take care of the energy of anger when it arises and to recognize and transform the seeds of anger that lie deep in my consciousness. When anger comes up, I am determined not to do or say anything, but to practice mindful breathing or mindful walking and acknowledge, embrace, and look deeply into my anger. I will learn to look with the eyes of compassion on those I think are the cause of my anger.

The Seventh Mindfulness Training:
Dwelling Happily in the Present Moment
Aware that life is available only in the present moment
and that it is possible to live happily in the here and
now, I am committed to training myself to live deeply
each moment of daily life. I will try not to lose myself
in dispersion or be carried away by regrets about the
past, worries about the future, or craving, anger or
jealousy in the present. I will practice mindful breathing
to come back to what is happening in the present
moment. I am determined to learn the art of mindful
living by touching the wondrous, refreshing, and healing
elements that are inside and around me, and by
nourishing seeds of joy, peace, love, and understanding
in myself, thus facilitating the work of transformation
and healing in my consciousness.

The Eighth Mindfulness Training:
Community and Communication
Aware that lack of communication always brings separa-
tion and suffering, I am committed to training myself in
the practice of compassionate listening and loving
speech. I will learn to listen deeply without judging or
reacting and refrain from uttering words that can create
discord or cause the community to break. I will make
every effort to keep communications open and to
reconcile and resolve all conflicts, however small.

The Ninth Mindfulness Training:
Truthful and Loving Speech
Aware that words can create suffering or happiness,
I am committed to learning to speak truthfully and
constructively, using only words that inspire hope and
confidence. I am determined not to say untruthful
things for the sake of personal interest or to impress
people, nor to utter words that might cause division or
hatred. I will not spread news that I do not know to be
certain nor criticize or condemn things of which I am
not sure. I will do my best to speak out about situations
of injustice, even when doing so may threaten my safety.

The Tenth Mindfulness Training:
Protecting the Sangha
Aware that the essence and aim of a Sangha is the
practice of understanding and compassion, I am
determined not to use the Buddhist community for
personal gain or profit or to transform our community
into a political instrument. A spiritual community
should, however, take a clear stand against oppression
and injustice and should strive to change the situation
without engaging in partisan conflicts.

The Eleventh Mindfulness Training:
Right Livelihood
Aware that great violence and injustice have been done
to the environment and society, I am committed not to
live with a vocation that is harmful to humans and
nature. I will do my best to select a livelihood that helps

realize my ideal of understanding and compassion.
Aware of global economic, political, and social realities,
I will behave responsibly as a consumer and as a citizen,
not investing in companies that deprive others of their
chance to live.

The Twelfth Mindfulness Training:
Reverence for Life
Aware that much suffering is caused by war and conflict,
I am determined to cultivate non-violence,
understanding, and compassion in my daily life and
to promote peace education, mindful mediation, and
reconciliation within families, communities, nations,
and in the world. I am determined not to kill and not
to let others kill. I will diligently practice deep looking
with my Sangha to discover better ways to protect life
and prevent war.

The Thirteenth Mindfulness Training: Generosity
Aware of the suffering caused by exploitation, social
injustice, stealing and oppression, I am committed to
cultivating loving-kindness and learning ways to work
for the well being of people, animals, plants, and
minerals. I will practice generosity by sharing my time,
energy, and material resources with those who are in
need. I am determined not to steal and not to possess
anything that should belong to others. I will respect
the property of others, but will try to prevent others
from profiting from human suffering or from the
suffering of other beings.

The Fourteenth Mindfulness Training:
Right Conduct

For lay members: Aware that sexual relations motivated
by craving cannot dissipate the feeling of loneliness,
but will create more suffering, frustration, and isolation,
I am determined not to engage in sexual relations
without mutual understanding, love and a long-term
commitment. In sexual relations, I must be aware of
future suffering that may be caused. I know that to
preserve the happiness of myself and others, I must
respect the rights and commitments of myself and
others. I will do everything in my power to protect
children from sexual abuse and to protect couples
and families from being broken by sexual misconduct.
I will treat my body with respect and preserve my vital
energies (sexual, breath, spirit) for the realization of
my bodhisattva ideal. I will be fully aware of the responsibility for bringing new lives in the world, and will
meditate on the world into which we bring new beings.

THE THREE BASKETS

The Buddhist collection of religious writing is known
collectively as Tripitaka in Sanskrit, and Tipitaka in Pali.
These terms mean "three baskets" and refer to the three
main categories within the canon, which is considered
to be directly transmitted from the Buddha. The three
categories include the Sutra Pitaka (doctrine), Vinaya
Pitaka (monastic discipline), and the Abhidharma Pitaka
(subtle philosophy). The sutras and the vinaya of all

Buddhist schools contain a huge number and variety of documents, including discourses on the dharma, commentary on teachings, worldly texts, and jataka tales (i.e., stories of the Buddha's lives and births).

Although Buddha never referenced the Three Baskets as a concept in his teaching, he did create the Vinaya. Others wrote the sutras by collecting the sayings and discourses of the Buddha. In addition, the Abhidhamma, or commentary Pitaka, are an organized philosophical systematization of the Buddha's teaching.

Almost all of these texts were originally composed in Sanskrit or Pali and then translated to Tibetan, Chinese, other Asian languages, and, eventually, English. When they were first written, the words were carved in stone, but these days they can be found easily on the Internet.

History of the Texts

The most notable set of texts from the early period is the Pali Canon, which was preserved in Sri Lanka by the Theravada School of Buddhism. The sutras it contains are part of the canon of every other Buddhist school.

Buddhist texts come in a huge variety of shapes and sizes. Some were carved into blocks, and others were written painstakingly on parchment. The earliest Buddhist writings ever found were fragments written on birch bark that dated to the first century. They were found in northwest Pakistan.

Note again, however, that Buddhists do not place as much value on the written word and on texts as believers of other religions. In fact, some practitioners dismiss any text as a false representation of the reality of Buddha and his teachings.

THE TEXTS

Texts can be divided up in many ways, but the most fundamental division is between canonical and non-canonical texts. The former, also called the Sutras, are believed to be, either literally or metaphorically, the actual words of the Buddha. The latter are the various commentaries on canonical texts, other treatises on the dharma, and collections of quotes and histories. Many of the texts fall into more than one category.

Each Buddhist school has its own belief about which texts are canonical and, further, each school contains various numbers and types of texts. The Theravada and other Nikaya schools believe, more or less literally, that these texts contain the actual words of the Buddha. The Theravada canon, also known as the Pali Canon after the language it was written in, contains some four million words.

Later texts, such as the Mahayana Sutras, are also considered to be the words of the Buddha, but they were transmitted either in secret, via lineages of mythical beings (such as the Nagas), or came directly

from other buddhas or bodhisattvas. Some 600
Mahayana Sutras have survived in Sanskrit, as well
as in Chinese and Tibetan.

The Six Perfections
The ninth century Indian Buddhist Shantideva is a
favorite of the fourteenth Dalai Lama. It begins with
an elaborate ritual worship section, but it further
explains the Six Perfections:

1. Generosity

2. Ethical discipline

3. Patience

4. Enthusiastic effort

5. Concentration

6. Wisdom

To become a buddha, a disciple must cultivate
The Six Perfections. Practicing the first four Perfections
creates discipline in all actions. The fourth Perfection,
enthusiastic effort, is necessary for the success of all
the Perfections. According to the law of karma, positive
actions then further cultivate the fifth perfection,
concentration, which creates serenity in the mind.
Wisdom, the sixth perfection, enables the mind to
understand reality as it was meant to be understood.
Then Enlightenment is impossible.

Like the Eightfold Path, the Six Perfections are not
necessarily progressive; also, they are in this order for
a reason. The Perfections go from basics to the most

elevated—in other words, from the general to the subtle. As you progress on the path, the practices grow in significance and difficulty. Each practice builds on the success of the previous one. In other words, the practice of each is impossible without the cultivation of the preceding one.

For example, when someone practices generosity, that person will naturally be able to accept the significance and necessity of ethical discipline. Ethical discipline then gives birth to patience. When people can be patient, they lose their impatience and thus have energy to be enthusiastic and focus their energies properly. When people spend their energy in good, happy ways, then they will be able to concentrate mindfully and focus. Then, when someone is able to concentrate mindfully, they will have the power to perfectly realize the Buddha nature of all phenomena and become as wise is as necessary for Enlightenment.

Bodhisattvas

The practice of the Perfections also benefits other people, not only oneself, which is the goal of a bodhisattva. Bodhisattvas are the ideal practitioners of the Six Perfections because their goal is to attain Enlightenment for the sake of all living beings. Indeed, "The 37 Practices of Bodhisattvas" explain that a bodhisattva should make the six transcendent Perfections her habits. Therefore, all physical, verbal, and mental behaviors and actions must support that goal.

In the Mahayana teachings, the bodhisattva's

practice stands as the example for all human beings in terms of goals and behavior. Their aim is unselfish: It is ultimate happiness for all living beings. Their motivation is to attain Enlightenment and to become buddhas for the Enlightenment and benefit of all living beings, and they maintain their unselfish desire at all times. The importance of the boddhisattva is one of the defining aspects of Mahayana Buddhism.

Schools of Buddhism

THERAVADA BUDDHISM

There is only one branch of Buddhism that claims to be directly descended from the sangha of the Buddha himself. The Theravada, which means Doctrine of the Elders, is sometimes called Southern Buddhism because its practitioners live mostly in Thailand, Burma, Sri Lanka, Cambodia, and Laos.

The Theravada are traditional and conservative. They don't put as much emphasis as other schools on texts that aren't directly related to the Buddha. Of course, considering its diverse locations, not every Theravadan Buddhist practices in the same way.

One of the most important people in Theravadan history is the emperor Ashoka, who first combined his empire with his religious beliefs. This helped create governmental institutions with a Buddhist influence through Southern Asia. In fact, the history of Sri Lanka is intimately connected with the development of Theravada Buddhism. Another of the more important aspects of Theravada Buddhism is its acceptance of devas, or spirits.

The Theravada also make clear distinctions between members of the monastic community and lay people, believing that monks and nuns should focus on meditation and lay people should use good deeds to help improve their karma. This is a traditional view, and certainly many people, both Theravadan and not, have taken up meditation with an eye toward nirvana.

Theravada Buddhists believe that everyone has the capacity to become Enlightened if only they would behave themselves, meditate a lot, purify their karma, and commit themselves to becoming Enlightened.

MAHAYANA BUDDHISM

During the first century CE, Buddhism went through many changes as it was adapted by all of the Asian cultures it had reached. It became so different from the original teachings that a new name for the school was coined. This new variation of Buddhism was called Mahayana, or Great Vehicle. At that time, the other schools came to be known as Hinayana, or Lesser Vehicle, although that term is no longer used.

Mahayana missionaries traveled through China, Japan, Mongolia, and Tibet. Today, Mahayana remains the most common form of Buddhism in China, Japan, Korea, Vietnam and Singapore.

Its adherents claimed that its school was based on words uttered by the Buddha but only discovered at the time of the school's development. Its goals and practices were decidedly different from the original teachings of the Buddha. For example, in Mahayana Buddhism, everyone is considered to be Enlightened already— the trick is realizing you're already Enlightened.

In addition, although boddhisattvas had existed previously in Buddhist thought, and, in fact, about four or five buddhas were believed to have lived during the time of the Buddha alone, it was only when Mahayana came into being that Buddhists began to rely on boddhisattvas to live as examples to other Buddhists.

Mahayana Texts
The Mahayana collection of texts, written in Buddhist Hybrid Sanskrit, includes the Perfection of Wisdom Sutras, the Avatatsaka, the Lotus Sutra, the Vimalakirti Sutra, and the Nirvana Sutra. This canon expanded further when Buddhists traveled to China and the texts were translated. In return, new texts were written so that the East Asian philosophies could combine with the Indian tradition.

Because of the unreliable beginnings of so many new texts, today's Buddhists consider most of these works less than reliable. However, some texts, such as the Platform Sutra and the Sutra of Perfect Enlightenment, were never thought to be authentic teachings, so they

are simply accepted as valid interpretations of the
original canon.

Other important texts of this movement include
the Samadhi Sutras, which focus on the attainment of
profound states of consciousness reached in meditation.
The Triskandha Sutra and the Suvarnaprabhasa Sutra
(or Golden Light Sutra) focus on the importance of
confessing faults. This sutra was significant because in
later years, in Japan, the Emperors used its words and
teachings to legitimize their rule, and it actually
provided a model for their government policies.

Early in the twentieth century, a collection of texts
was found in a mound near Gilgit, Afghanistan.
Amongst them was the Ajitasena Sutra, which, because
no antagonism exists toward the Hinayana in it, appears
to be a mixture of Mahayana and pre-Mahayana ideals.
This new teaching involves an arahant seeing all the
Buddha fields. Legend (or instruction) says that by
reciting the name of the sutra, a disciple can save all
beings from suffering and the hell realms. It also says
that meditative practice enables the practitioner to
see with the eyes of a Buddha.

VAJRAYANA BUDDHISM

In approximately 500 CE, another, more physical form
of Buddhism developed in India. This practice was
called tantra, and the texts are called the Buddhist
tantras. This school of Buddhism was called Vajrayana.

Vajrayana relies on ritual and the physical body to

stimulate the spirituality. The intention of the Vajrayana
School was the same as that of as the other Buddhist
schools: to reach Enlightenment. The method, however,
was different. Rather than relying on knowledge of the
scripture and living a monastic life or on perfecting
meditation, members of the Vajrayana School turned
to ritual on their path.

Vajrayana Buddhism is completely entwined with
the history of Buddhism in Tibet, where it is predominant. Other large populations of this Buddhist school
are found in Mongolia, portions of Siberia, and portions
of India, especially areas bordering Tibet.

Vajrayana Texts
Before performing the ritual practices, however,
a Vajrayana monk must first become knowledgeable
about many texts. The canon of the Vajrayana schools
includes many related texts related to Nikaya (i.e., the
Tibetan Buddhist canonical text), as well as Mahayana
sutras. However, the specifically Vajrayana texts most
strongly characterize this school. These texts are
considered to be the word of the Buddha, and the
Tibetan Canon contains translations of almost 500
tantras and more than 2000 commentaries on them.
These texts are typically concerned with elaborate
rituals and meditations.

A late Tibetan tradition has classified these texts:

Kriya tantras. These form a large subgroup that
appeared between the second and the sixth centuries

CE. The Kriya tantras focus on actions (i.e., ritual, etc.). Each centers around a particular buddha or bodhisattva, and many are based around dharanis (i.e., mantras).

Carya tantras. This small class of texts probably emerged after the sixth century. It centers entirely on the worship of the buddha Vairocana, the main wisdom buddha.

Other Vajrayana Literature

The Sadhanamala is a collection of Sadhanas or spiritual practices. Vajrayana adepts, known as siddhas, often expounded their teachings in the form of songs. Collections of these songs—such as the Caryagiti, which is a collection of songs by various siddhas—are popular. The Dohakosha is a collection of songs by the siddha Saraha from the ninth century. A collection known in English as "The Hundred Thousand Songs" of Milarepa is also popular.

Kukai, who started Shingon Buddhism, wrote multiple treatises on Vajrayana Buddhism, which are distinctive to his school.

Tantra

Tantra can only be taught and practiced by experienced monks and priests—people cannot practice Vajrayana Buddhism on their own. The gurus in this school are called tulkas, and they are often treated as deities, with followers believing that they return to life again and again in order to teach others. Chogyam Trungpa is a present-day tulka with this royal spiritual lineage. (Note that despite being Tibetan, The Dalai Lama is not a Tantric Buddhist.)

Ritual Practices

The first ritual practice is prostration. During this practice, a person lies in front of a Buddhist shrine and stands up. He repeats this 10,000 times in a row. Some rituals must be done 100,000 times.

These rituals are practiced in a specific order and under specific directions of a monk. The point is that they take years of perfection and, when performed together, are believed to be a sure path to Enlightenment. If a person missteps along the way, however, he or she is destined to become a deva in a level of hell.

During an initiation, a guru will select a yidam, or personal deity, for his student. The guru will also offer his student a mantra (chant) to encourage his meditation practice. Finally, the guru and his student will commit to creating a mandala together. This complex drawing, often created with colored grains of sand, is a sacred road map that describes the journey the student will take to reach the yidam. Through these and many other rituals, a student will dissolve his own identity into that of the ultimate reality and achieve nirvana.

TIBETAN BUDDHISM

The Indian teachers Padmasambhava and Shantarakshita brought Buddhism to Tibet in the eighth century, although it was later nearly destroyed by Lang Darma, a Tibetan King devoted to Bön, the pre-Buddhist religion of Tibet. Then, in the eleventh century, Tibet's king invited Atisha, a Buddhist monk, to come from India to teach a dharma that everyone could understand and practice and that would show how all of Buddha's teachings could be integrated. In response, Atisha composed the instructions on lamrim (i.e., the stages of the path to Enlightenment in Tibetan Buddhism).

Following this journey, Atisha and his principal disciple, Dromtonpa, established what is known as the Kadampa tradition. It was later revived by the Tibetan teacher Je Tsongkhapa, the founder of the Gelugpa, or New Kadampa, tradition.

Tibet's longstanding and colorful national Buddhist practice is less philosophical than other branches. Indeed, Tibetans managed to merge its ancient native practices with the ascetic Buddhist tradition to create what can only be described as a joyful school of Buddhism. Tibetan Buddhism is an offshoot of the Vajrayana School, and its chief figure is the Dalai Lama.

A defining feature of Tibetan Buddhism is that Enlightenment is not only possible in one lifetime, but that it could actually be achieved in an instant, based on extraordinary acts and achievements. Tibetan Buddhists believe that each individual has a specific path that he or she must follow and can encompass the entire path in one lifetime.

Since 1950, when Tibet was overrun by communist China, the occupying country has been attempting to destroy all traces of the culture's Buddhist practice.

Tibetan Buddhist Canon

The Tibetan Canon, which belongs to the various schools of Tibetan Vajrayana Buddhism, contains the earlier three classes of texts, the tantric texts, and commentaries on them. In fact, the most thorough collection of Mahayana sutras is found in the Tibetan canon. Some of the texts are actually attributed to the Buddha, and others are recognized as commentaries by Buddhist lamas, or teachers.

Tibetan Buddhism also has a unique and special class of texts called terma, which were composed long ago but hidden in caves and then destined to be rediscovered at a later date. Tertön are the monks destined to discovered these terma. A further school of thought is of "mind termas," which are "discovered" in the mind of the tertön. The Nyingma school, which include Tibetan Buddhist schools and a famous Buddhist center of learning, has a large terma literature, and many of the terma texts are believed to have been written by Padmasambhava, who is particularly important to the Nyingmas.

Probably the best-known terma text is the "Tibetan Book of the Dead," which was published to great acclaim in the twentieth century.

PURE LAND BUDDHISM

Although other Buddhist schools rely on ritual

(Vajrayana) and monastic practices (Theravada) to guide them on their paths, Pure Land Buddhists believe that faith is the predominant force on the way to Enlightenment—which means that the majority of Buddhists who get married, have jobs and careers, and have children practice this form of Buddhism because it doesn't require endless hours of meditation, ritual, or leading a monastic life.

The other aspect of Pure Land Buddhism that makes it attractive to lay people is its belief in another "purer" world or universe that allows for greater Enlightenment possibilities. Pure Land Buddhists believe that since the time of the Buddha, this world has become more corrupt and further from a global Enlightenment; they believe that the goal of their practice is to be reborn into another world.

The Pure Land School discusses three major sutras: the Infinite Life Sutra, also known as the Larger Pure Land Sutra; the Amitabha Sutra, also known as the Smaller Pure Land Sutra; and the Contemplation Sutra, or Visualization Sutra. These works illustrate the Pure Land in which a specific Buddha named Amitabha resides. When he was a bodhisattva, Amitabha took forty-six vows to build a Pure Land in which everyone could practice the dharma without difficulty or distraction (i.e., no matter what class they were or how much time or money they had). The sutras explain that anyone can be reborn if they conduct themselves purely and have great faith. Thinking continuously of Amitabha, praising him, recounting his virtues, and

chanting his name are also definitive ways to reach
the Pure Land.

ZEN BUDDHISM

The Chinese word Ch'an is derived from the Sanskrit
word that means meditation, which is just what Ch'an
(or, in Japanese, Zen) Buddhism is: an intensely meditative form of Buddhism that began to develop in fifth
century China. It spread to Japan, eventually, and, as it
continued to move westward, more people began to
know it by its Japanese name.

In some ways, Zen Buddhism stands apart from
other Buddhist schools because it seeks to loosen the
hold that too much thinking can create on the mind. In
the same way that exercise can loosen and then re-align
the body, Zen teaching aims to relax the mind, which
then allows it to grow stronger in its Buddhist practice.
Zen Buddhists do not practice traditional, logical ways
of thinking and learning about samsara and
Enlightenment. Rather, Zen Buddhists believe that logic
ultimately leads to confusion because it removes the
thinker from the being and the ability to exist in a
simple, uninterpreted experience.

The Asian masters who developed Zen Buddhism
paved the way for modern existentialists and philosophers, such as Nietzsche and Wittgenstein, who developed their philosophies of "nothingness" in Europe.
Zen was originally misunderstood by Westerners, who
took it to be a dispassionate philosophy that espoused

nothingness over meaning, but, in reality, this embrace of "emptiness" (i.e., an open and willing mind) is meant to bring a practitioner to a higher state of awareness and being.

Zen monks often practice quiet and methodical habits, such as gardening, to cultivate a serene and open mind. Also, they are known for practicing a particular type of meditation called zazen, during which a meditator sit with crossed legs and attempts to empty the mind of all thoughts. Meditators want to be aware of their bodies but allow their minds to expand while, at the same time, not focusing on any ideas or on any one thing outside of themselves.

The Zen school is also famous for using koans to teach its philosophy. A koan is a short story or question that has no real meaning or answer. Its purpose is to distract the questioner from a logical train of thought. One such question is, "What is the sound of one hand clapping?" Mind emptying allows someone to be open and receptive to the truth of Enlightenment.

PART THREE

Buddhism in the World

"THE BUDDHA SAID, 'SALVATION DOES NOT COME FROM THE SIGHT OF ME. IT DEMANDS STRENUOUS EFFORT AND PRACTICE. SO WORK HARD AND SEEK YOUR OWN SALVATION DILIGENTLY.' "

—Jamyang Jamtsho Wangchuk
as the Dalai Lama in *Seven Years in Tibet* (1997)

Buddhism Timeline

Fifth Century BCE—First Buddhist Council
Three months after the death of the Buddha, the first
council convenes to record the Buddha's sayings (sutras)
and define the monastic rules (vinaya). Maha Kassapa,
the most respected and elderly arahant, presides at the
Council. Ananda, the Buddha's main disciple and cousin,
recites the Buddha's discourses while Upali, another
disciple, recites the rules of the vinaya. These become
the basis of the Pali Canon, the main Buddhist text.

The arahants unanimously agree that within the
sangha (community), nothing the Buddha said should
be changed, and that the arahants should introduce no
new teachings in the future. There is very little record of
this meeting, but experts believe that there is no conflict
about what the Buddha taught.

The teachings are divided into various parts, and
each section is assigned to an elder and his pupils so
they can commit the teachings to memory. Nothing is
written down—indeed, the Pali Canon remains oral for
centuries. These groups of people work together and
check with each other to make sure no omissions or
additions occur.

383 BCE—Second Buddhist Council
One hundred years after the first council, following
conflicts between two groups of Buddhist students,

a council is called to create harmony between the two schools. No one is arguing about the dharma, however—just about the vinaya.

One school believes that the Buddha was a human being who reached Enlightenment and that this Enlightenment can really only be attained by monks who follow the monastic rules and practice the teaching for the sake of overcoming suffering and attaining arahantship. Meanwhile, the other group, the Mahayana, relax the monastic rules so that they appeal to more people, including both monks and lay people. For this reason, their name, Mahayana, means "great" or "majority."

Nothing resolves for the groups, so more splinter sects are created.

250 BCE — Third Buddhist Council

The Mauryan king Ashoka (273–232 BCE) converts to Buddhism after using brutal force to take over much of the territory in Eastern India. Regretful of the horrors for which he is responsible, the king decides to renounce violence. He begins to promote Buddhism by building stupas (i.e., Buddhist shrines that often contain a relic or at least some scriptural text) and pillars that urge respect for all life, both human and animal, and to encourage everyone in his dominion to follow the dharma. He also builds roads and hospitals around the country.

This period marks the first spread of Buddhism beyond India. In it, the king sends emissaries for that purpose, and spreads Buddhism as far as the Greek kingdoms in the West—in particular, the neighboring Greco-Bactrian Kingdom—and possibly even farther, to the Mediterranean.

Then, in the third century BCE, the Third Council convenes under the patronage of Emperor Ashoka in order to help establish an official agreement on the dharma and the vinaya. The idea is for this to create a cohesive sangha, and The Three Jewels would be complete. At the council, however, various individuals and groups dispute much of what the Buddha taught about the vinaya and the dharma. Thus, the chairman of the council, Moggaliputta Tissa, compiles a book called the Kathavatthu.

Moggaliputta Tissa designs the book to refute any of the arguments that are being put forth, and the official council agrees to endorse Moggaliputta and his version of Buddhism as orthodox. Emperor Ashoka then declares this form of Buddhism to be his empire's official religion. This school of thought is called Vibhajjavada, a Pali word that means "Teaching of Analysis."

The version of the scriptures officially adopted at the Third Council includes the vinaya, sutra, and the Abhidhamma commentaries, which are now officially and collectively known as Tripitaka (Three Baskets). Emperor Ashoka's son, the Venerable Mahinda, and some fellow monks take these works to Sri Lanka so that they can be written down in Pali. This is the first time the Buddha's teachings are put on paper.

185 BCE
The Sunga Empire begins persecution
against Buddhism
After murdering King Brhadrata, the last Mauryan
ruler, about fifty years after Ashoka died, the military
commander-in-chief Pusyamitra Sunga takes the throne
and establishes the Sunga dynasty (185–73 BCE). Sunga
is an orthodox Brahman known for his hostility toward
and persecution of Buddhists. He destroys 84,000
Buddhist stupas and monasteries and offers 100 gold
coins for the head of each Buddhist monk. He also
oversees the conversion of hundreds of Buddhist
monasteries to Hindu temples, including those in such
Buddhist holy places as Nalanda, Bodhgaya, Sarnath,
and Mathura.

185–73 BCE
Demetrius creates a Pro-Buddhist kingdom
In 180 BEC, the Greco-Bactrian king Demetrius I
invades India as far as Pataliputra, thus establishing an
Indo-Greek kingdom that lasts until the end of the first
century BCE. Buddhism flourishes under him and
under the Indo-Greek kings after him. In that way, he
shows support for the previous Mauryan empire and
helps to protect the Buddhist faith from further religious
persecution by the Sungas.

68
The Buddhist White Horse Temple in China is founded

78–101
The Fourth Buddhist council
The Kushan emperor Kanishka convenes the Fourth Council in Kashmir, India, around 100 CE. Because those who now rule Theravada Buddhism do not recognize the authenticity of this council, this period begins the formal rise of Mahayana Buddhism. It is sometimes called "the council of heretical monks."

Kanishka gathers 500 Bhikkhus, including the arahant Vasumitra, to edit the Tripitaka and to add to it more references and remarks. Then, according to Mahayana doctrine, a set of new scriptures is approved to support this new way of thinking about Buddhism. The new scriptures are written in Sanskrit, which further helps to communicate Buddhist thought to the rest of the world.

200s
During and after the second century, the important Buddhist monks Nagarjuna, Asanga, Shantideva, Ashvagosha, and Vasubandhu create writings to support various versions of the Mahayana vision so that it becomes the leading form of Buddhism.

300s
Buddhist monks travel to Korea.

400s
Earliest evidence of Buddhism in Myanmar and Indonesia. The major stupa at Dambulla in Sri Lanka is constructed.

403

In China, Buddhist monks are told that they do not have to bow to the emperor.

475

Bodhidharma founds the Chan school at the Shaolin Temple of Zen Buddhism.

500s

Zen monks go to Vietnam. Jataka stories are translated into Persian.

552

Buddhism is introduced in Japan.

671

Chinese Buddhist pilgrim Yi Jing visits Palembang, capital of the partly Buddhist kingdom of Srivijaya on the island of Sumatra, Indonesia, and reports more than 1000 Buddhist monks in residence. Uisang returns to Korea after studying Chinese Huayan Buddhism and founds the Hwaeom school.

736

Huayan is transmitted to Japan via Korea, when Ryben invites the Korean Hwaeom monk Simsang to lecture and formally founds Japan's Kegon tradition in the Tÿdaiji temple.

743–754

The Chinese monk Jianzhen attempts to reach Japan eleven times, succeeding in 754 to establish the Japanese Ritsu school, which specializes in the vinaya (monastic rules).

700s

Jataka stories are translated to Syriac and Arabic. An account of Buddha's life is translated into Greek by John of Damascus and widely circulated to Christians as the story of Barlaam and Josaphat. By the 1300s, this story of Josaphat has become so popular that Josaphat (who some people believe is Buddha) is made a Catholic saint.

700s

Under the reign of King Trisong Deutsen, Padmasambhava travels from Afghanistan to establish tantric Buddhism in Tibet, replacing Bonpo as the kingdom's main religion. Buddhism quickly spreads to Sikkhim and Bhutan.

760

Borobodur, the famous Indonesian Buddhist structure, starts to be constructed. It is completed in 830, after about fifty years of work.

804

Emperor Kammu of Japan sends a fleet of four ships to mainland China (only two of which arrive) with the Vajrayana monk Kukai and another monk, Saichÿ, both of whom return to Japan to found Buddhist schools.

841–846

The Tang Dynasty in China prohibits the practice of Buddhism. Indian Buddhism declines, too, because of persecution by King Langdharma in India.

900s

Buddhist temple construction commences at Pagan, Myanmar, while in Tibet, there is a strong Buddhist revival. Dongshan Liangjie and Caoshan Benji found The Caodong school of Zen in southern China.

971

The Chinese Song Dynasty commissions wood carvers in Chengdu to carve the entire Buddhist canon for printing. They produce 130,000 blocks of writing that can be used for publishing the canon. They complete the work in 983.

991

A printed copy of the Song Dynasty Buddhist canon arrives in Korea, and the government begins to consider Buddhism as a viable state religion.

1009

Vietnam's Ly Dynasty begins, partly brought about by an official political alliance with Buddhist monks.

1010
Korea begins carving its own woodblock print edition
of the Buddhist canon. No completion date is known.
The canon is continuously expanded with the arrival
of new texts from China.

1025
Srivijaya, a kingdom with a recognized Buddhist ethic
based in Sumatra, is raided by pirates from southern
India. Srivijaya survives but declines in importance.

1044–1077
In Burma, King Anoratha converts the country to
Theravada Buddhism with the aid of monks and books
from Sri Lanka.

1057
Anawrahta of Myanmar captures part of northern
Thailand, bringing Theravada Buddhism into the country.

1063
A copy of the Pali Canon arrives in Korea from China.

1084–1113
In Myanmar, King Kyanzittha (son of Anawrahta)
completes the building of the Shwezigon pagoda,
a shrine for relics of the Buddha, including a tooth
brought from Sri Lanka. The inscriptions throughout
the shrine refer to him as an incarnation of Vishnu,
a chakravartin, a bodhisattva, and a dharmaraja.

1100–1125

The Chinese Song Dynasty outlaws Buddhism
to promote Taoism.

1133–1212

Honen Shonin establishes Pure Land Buddhism
in Japan.

1181

A Mahayana Buddhist, Bodhisattva Jayavarman VII,
assumes control of the Khmer kingdom. He constructs
the Bayon, the most prominent Buddhist structure
in the Angkor temple complex. This sets the stage
for the future conversion of the Khmer people
to Theravada Buddhism.

1190

In Myanmar, a new regime adapts Burmese Buddhism
to more closely resemble Sri Lankan Theravada schools.

Late 1100s

The great Buddhist educational center at Nalanda
is destroyed by the Turks.

1200s

Theravada overtakes Mahayana as the dominant form
of Buddhism in Cambodia. Thailand and Sri Lanka
influence this change for political reasons.

1238

The Thai Kingdom of Sukhothai is established.
It institutes Theravada Buddhism as the state religion.

1287
The Theravada kingdom in Myanmar falls to the Mongols.

1391–1474
Gyalwa Gendun Drubpa becomes the first Dalai Lama of Tibet.

1600–1700
Vietnam divided, the South chooses to support Mahayana Buddhism as the official ideology of their kingdom.

1614
The Toyotomi family rebuilds a great image of Buddha at the Temple of Hokoji in Kyoto.

1642
Guushi Khan of the Khoshuud donates the sovereignty of Tibet to the fifth Dalai Lama.

1800s
In Thailand, King Mongkut—himself a former monk—reforms and modernizes the monkhood. This movement continues into the twenty-first century under the inspiration of several ascetic monks.

1802–1820
Nguyen Anh comes to the throne of Vietnam (which is now united) and forbids adult men to attend Buddhist ceremonies.

1860

In Sri Lanka, the monastic and lay communities bring about a major revival of Buddhism, hand in hand with a growing nationalism political movement. Continuing until the present day, Buddhism flourishes in this country, and Sri Lankan monks and expatriate lay people have been prominent in spreading Theravada Buddhism in Asia, the West, and Africa.

1879

A council convenes under the patronage of King Mindon of Burma to re-write and re-edit the Pali canon. The king has the texts engraved on 729 stones, which are then set upright on the grounds of a monastery near Mandalay.

1880s

In Sri Lanka, the international Buddhist flag is designed with the assistance of Henry Steele Olcott (a formidable American religious figure). The World Fellowship of Buddhists later adopts it as a symbol.

1893

World Parliament of Religions meets in Chicago, IL, with Buddhism featured.

1896

Nepalese archaeologists rediscover the great stone pillar of Ashoka at Lumbini.

1899
Gordon Douglas is ordained in Myanmar. He is the first Westerner to be ordained in the Theravada tradition.

1949
Mahabodhi Temple in Bodh Gaya is returned to partial Buddhist control.

1950
World Fellowship of Buddhists is founded in Colombo, Sri Lanka.

1956
Indian Untouchable leader B. R. Ambedkar converts to Buddhism with more than 350,000 followers, beginning the modern Neo-Buddhist movement.

1956
The Zen Studies Society is founded in New York to support the work of D.T. Suzuki.

1956
The 2,500th anniversary of the Buddha's birth is celebrated in New Delhi.

1957
Caves near the summit of Pai-tai mountain, Fangshan district, southwest of Beijing, are re-opened, revealing thousands of Buddhist sutras that were carved onto stone sometime around the seventh century. Seven sets of rubbings are made. This work takes two years.

1959

Together with some 100,000 Tibetans, the fourteenth Dalai Lama flees the Chinese occupation of Tibet and establishes an exile community in India. The Chinese invaders completely destroy all monasteries but a handful and severely persecute Buddhist practitioners.

1962

Shunryu Suzuki founds the San Francisco Zen Center.

1965

The Burmese government arrests more than 700 monks for refusing to accept government rule.

1966

World Buddhist Sangha Council is convened by Theravadins in Sri Lanka in the hopes of bridging differences and working together. It is attended by leading monks from many countries and many sects.

The attendees unanimously approve nine points written by Venerable Walpola Rahula:

The Buddha is our only Master.

We take refuge in the Buddha, the dharma, and the sangha (The Three Jewels).

We do not believe that this world is created and ruled by a God.

We consider that the purpose of life is to develop compassion for all living beings without discrimination and to work for their good, happiness, and peace; and to develop wisdom leading to the realization of Ultimate Truth.

We accept the Four Noble Truths, namely dukkha suffering), the arising of dukkha, the cessation of dukkha, and the Path leading to the cessation of dukkha; and the law of cause and effect (Pratitya-samutpada).

All conditioned things (samskara) are impermanent (anitya) and dukkha, and that all conditioned and unconditioned things (dharma) are without self (anatman).

We accept the Thirty-seven Qualities conducive to Enlightenment (called bodhipaksadharma) as different aspects of the Path taught by the Buddha leading to Enlightenment.

There are three ways of attaining bodhi or Enlightenment—as a disciple (sraavaka), as a Pratyeka-Buddha, and as a Samyak-sam-Buddha (perfectly and Fully Enlightened Buddha). We accept it as the highest, noblest, and most heroic to follow the career of a bodhisattva and to become a Samyak-sam-Buddha in order to save others.

We admit that in different countries there are differences regarding Buddhist beliefs and practices. These external forms and expressions should not be confused with the essential teachings of the Buddha.

1975

Lao Communist rulers attempt to change attitudes regarding religion, in particular, calling on monks to work and not to beg. This causes many to return to lay life, although Buddhism remains popular without a strong monastic community.

1975

The Insight Meditation Society is established in Barre, MA.

1975–1979

Cambodian communists under Pol Pot try to completely destroy Buddhism and very nearly succeed. By the time the Vietnamese invade Cambodia in 1978, nearly every monk and religious intellectual has been either murdered or driven into exile, and nearly every temple and Buddhist library has been destroyed.

1978

In Burma, monks and novices are arrested, disrobed, and imprisoned by the government. Monasteries are closed and property seized. The famous and well-regarded monk U Nayaka is arrested and dies; the government claims that it was suicide.

2001

Afghanistan's Taliban rulers destroy two 2,000-year-old Buddhist statues they regard as insults to Islam. Numerous world governments try to intervene, but the Taliban deems them to be unholy toward Islam.

2004

In Sri Lanka, Buddhist monks acting as candidates
for the Jaathika Hela Urumaya party win nine seats
in elections.

2005

Three months after a devastating tsunami nearly
destroys large Buddhist populations in Sri Lanka,
Malaysia, and Thailand, as well as other Southeast Asian
countries, Buddhists from around the world meet
in Sri Lanka to launch an international relief organization. Olcott Gunasekera, President of the Asian Buddhist
Congress, says that the December 26, 2004, tsunami
experience highlights the urgent need for a Buddhist
relief organization.

The Story of Buddhism's Expansion into the World

Once the Buddha passed into parinirvana, it was up
to the sangha to figure out how to communicate and
spread his teachings. Researchers know very little about
the first few years after the Buddha's death because few
teachers or historians wrote at the time. However,
we do know that the sangha held a council very soon
after the Buddha's death to reach agreement on what

his teachings were and what would be best for the community. However, there is very little record of this meeting, nor does there seem to have been any definitive agreement reached.

A second council was held in 380 BCE to discuss the rules of monasticism and the qualities of the arahants. These disputes were never resolved and so began the divisions within Buddhism, with different groups of Buddhists declaring their beliefs and sanghas to be more authentic than those of other groups. Despite these disagreements, however, Buddhism still continued to spread slowly in India.

Two centuries after Buddha's death, India barely fought off Alexander the Great's attempt at world domination and, through enormous brutality, an emperor named Ashoka came to power. But Ashoka felt great remorse about the death and destruction he had caused, so he befriended a Buddhist monk and discussed his feelings.

He soon became a devotee of Buddhism and assimilated Buddhist philosophy into his political thinking. He sent ambassadors throughout his kingdom to spread the dharma. His "dharma" certainly wasn't the direct teaching of the Buddha because he wasn't only trying to help others find Enlightenment—he was also trying to support a government. Nevertheless, most Buddhist ruins date back to the Ashokan empire. The emperor built numerous monuments, and on all of them he had Buddhist history and art inscribed, which helped to communicate the Buddha's teachings over time.

Ashoka made pilgrimages to places where Buddha had lived and significant sites throughout the Buddha's journeys. He had his citizens search for Buddhist reliquaries, which he then had enshrined. People used these pieces as sites at which to pray and worship. He called them stupas. When Ashoka died, the region looked very different, as it was covered with Buddhist shrines, monasteries, and monuments.

Although Ashoka had great power, the Hellenistic world at that time formed an uninterrupted consolidation across the borders from India to Greece. Nevertheless, some of the Edicts of Ashoka that are inscribed on the stupas describe the efforts he made to spread the word of the Buddhist faith throughout the kingdom. The Edicts actually mention the names and location of the Greek monarchs who listened to the proselytizing of the monks. They include Antiochus II Theos of the Seleucid Kingdom (261–246 BCE), Ptolemy II Philadelphos of Egypt (285–247 BCE), Antigonus Gonatas of Macedonia (276–239 BCE), Magas of Cyrene (288–258 BCE), and Alexander of Epirus (272–255 BCE).

One stupa reads as follows: "The conquest by dharma has been won here, on the borders, and even six hundred yojanas (4,000 miles) away, where the Greek king Antiochos rules, beyond there where the four kings named Ptolemy, Antigonos, Magas and Alexander rule, likewise in the south among the Cholas, the Pandyas, and as far as Tamraparni." Furthermore, some of Ashoka's emissaries were actually Greek Buddhist monks who had already converted.

Many scholars have surmised that these inter-actions are evident not only in the stupas but in Hellenistic thought as well. Clement of Alexandria, for example, wrote about the Buddhism communities in his territory, and some believe that the pre-Christian monastic order Therapeutae may be derived from the Pali word "Theravada."

The missionary efforts of Ashoka that spread the faith into numerous Asian countries were largely successful. In fact, by the time of the Fourth Buddhist Council, expanding Buddhism was a goal of most of the sangha, regardless of the division, and by 200 BCE, Buddhism was the official religion of Sri Lanka.

In the area east of the Indian subcontinent (which is Myanmar today), Indian culture strongly influenced the group in control at the time, the Mons. The Mons converted to Buddhism around 200 BCE under King Ashoka. Early Mon Buddhist temples, such as Peikthano in central Burma, have been dated between the first and the fifth century CE. There is also a legend, which isn't mentioned on the edicts, that Ashoka sent a missionary to the north through the Himalayas.

Although Ashoka attempted to create a unified theory of Buddhism, his adoption of one school of thinking had the opposite affect. After 250 BCE, the Sthavira school, who had been rejected by the Third Council in favor of the Theravada tradition, and the

Dharmaguptaka school became quite influential in northwestern India and central Asia. Their prominence remained for a couple of centuries. The segmenting belief of the Dharmaguptakas was the idea that Buddha was separate, and above, the rest of the Buddhist community and that no one could ever reach him. This was an attempt to deify the Buddha. The Sthaviras, meanwhile, believed that past, present, and future are all simultaneous.

BUDDHISM SPREADS

Despite its being widespread through southern and central Asia, Buddhism began to wane in India after 500 CE. It nearly became extinct after about 1200 CE, partially due to Muslim invasions and partially due to Hindu revival movements. Over the years, however, Buddhism spread into Northern Asia, becoming an important religious force in China, Japan, Vietnam, Burma, Thailand, and Indonesia. Buddhists adapted their understanding of the religion to their particular country and to their region's history and culture, creating still other Buddhist schools and sects.

Buddhism began to be an accepted and well-regarded philosophy throughout the world in around 100 BCE. At that time, much of the Middle Eastern world began to use "star within a diadem" symbols, also called "eight-spoked wheels," which were considered to be influenced by the design of the Buddhist dharma wheel. These symbols appeared on the coins of the

Hebrew King Alexander Jannaeus (103–76 BCE), for example. Alexander Jannaeus was associated with the sect of the Sadducees and the monastic order of the Essenes, which were precursors of Christianity. These representations of eight-spoked wheels continued under the reign of his widow, Queen Alexandra, until the Roman invasion of Judea in 63 BCE. This proves, to scholars, some intermingling of the philosophies.

Buddhist gravestones from the Ptolemaic period have been found in Alexandria, decorated with depictions of the dharma wheel. The Buddhist art of the Mons was especially influenced by the Indian art of the Gupta and post-Gupta periods, and their mannerist style spread widely in Southeast Asia following the expansion of the Mon kingdom between the fifth and eighth centuries. The Theravada faith expanded in the northern parts of Southeast Asia under Mon influence, until it was progressively displaced by Mahayana Buddhism from around the sixth century CE.

During the first century CE, the development of the Silk Road brought about many changes and more complete communication throughout the Middle East and Asia. The Romans had conquered much of the area, and they had a seemingly unending desire for Asian luxury items. Trade on the overland Silk Road also revived the sea connections between the Mediterranean and China, with India as a regular stop along the way. Because of this, India began to more strongly influence Southeast Asian countries, as trade routes linked India with Burma, Thailand, Cambodia, and Vietnam.

Therefore, for more than a thousand years, Indian influence was the major factor that brought a certain level of cultural unity to the various countries of the region. Both Theravada and Mahayana Buddhism, as well as Brahmanism and Hinduism, were brought to these new regions.

And it wasn't just merchants who spread all of this new culture throughout the world—pilgrims did, too. Ashoka's son Mahinda and six companions proselytized in Sri Lanka during the second century BCE. They converted the king and many of the nobility, and they oversaw construction of the great Mahavihara monastery, a center of Sinhalese orthodoxy. The Pali Canon was printed in Sri Lanka during this time, and the Theravada tradition flourished there. The great Buddhist commentator Buddhaghosa also preached in this area during the fourth and through the turn of the fifth century.

SCHOOLS DIVERSIFY AND SOLIDIFY

Although Mahayana Buddhism gained some influence at that time, Theravada ultimately prevailed, and Sri Lanka turned out to be the last stronghold of Theravada Buddhism. From there, it would expand again to Southeast Asia from the eleventh century.

At around this time, one of the most famous Indo-Greek kings, Menander, who reigned from 160–135 BCE, converted to Buddhism. On the stupas, he is mentioned as one of the great benefactors of the

Mahayana Buddhist faith, similar to King Ashoka. Menander's coins have the inscription "Savior king" in Greek and "Great king of the dharma" in a Sanskrit-derivative. When he died, his remains were claimed by the cities under his rule and were enshrined in stupas.

Meanwhile, the interaction between Greek and Buddhist cultures may have had some influence on the evolution of Mahayana. Over time, this Buddhist school developed a more refined philosophical approach and played with the idea of Buddha as a "man-god," which is very much in line with the Greek concept of gods. Mahayans also believed that all people have a Buddha-nature inside them and should therefore aspire to Buddhahood, because it is an inherent possibility.

At the same time that Mahayana Buddhism was expanding, there were many complex political changes occurring in northwestern India. The societies in the area at this point were truly "Indo-Greek" kingdoms, and the governments eventually created the Kushan Empire in approximately 12 BCE. The Kushans supported Buddhism, and the group convened a fourth Buddhist council in approximately 100 CE in Kashmir. This council is directly responsible for the ascension of Mahayana Buddhism over (at the time) Theravada Buddhism. Of course, for their part, the arahants and monks associated with Theravada Buddhism did not recognize the authenticity of this council, so it was sometimes called "the Council of Heretical monks."

The Fourth Council was headed by Kaniska and gathered 500 bhikkhus (i.e., monks) in Kashmir to edit the Tripitaka and create a final version. Research has found that the group probably had to deal with approximately 300,000 verses. In the end, the group approved a brand-new set of scriptures, as well as fundamental principles of the Mahayana philosophy. Thus, the Theravadan school would not accept its teachings.

Expansion of Mahayana Buddhism continued between the first and the tenth century CE. From that point on, and in the space of a few centuries, Mahayana was to flourish and spread in the East from India to Southeast Asia and toward the north, to Central Asia, China, Korea, and, finally, to Japan in 538 CE.

BUDDHIST ART AND ARCHITECTURE

From the fifth to the thirteenth century, Southeast Asia had very powerful empires and became extremely active in Buddhist architectural and artistic creation. The main Buddhist influence now came directly by sea from the Indian subcontinent, so that these empires essentially followed the Mahayana faith. The Sri Vijaya Empire to the south and the Khmer Empire to the north competed for influence, and their art expressed the rich Mahayana pantheon of the bodhisattvas.

The Sri Vijayan empire, a maritime empire centered on the island of Sumatra in Indonesia, had adopted Mahayana and Vajrayana Buddhism under a line of rulers named the Sailendras. Sri-Vijaya spread Mahayana Buddhist art during its expansion in Southeast Asia. Numerous statues of Mahayana bodhisattvas from this period are characterized by a very strong refinement and technical sophistication and are found throughout the region. Extremely rich architectural remains are visible at the temple of Borobudur (the largest Buddhist structure in the world, built from around 780 CE) in Java, which has 505 images of the seated Buddha. This empire declined due to conflicts with the Chola rulers of India, before being destabilized by the Islamic expansion from the thirteenth century.

From the ninth to the thirteenth century, the Mahayana Buddhist and Hindu Khmer Empire dominated much of the Southeast Asian peninsula. Under the Khmer, more than 900 temples were built in Cambodia and in neighboring Thailand. Angkor was at the center of this development, with a temple complex and urban organization able to support around one million urban dwellers. One of the greatest Khmer kings, Jayavarman VII (1181–1219), built large Mahayana Buddhist structures at Bayon and Angkor Thom.

Following the destruction of Buddhism in mainland India during the eleventh century, Mahayana Buddhism declined in Southeast Asia, to be replaced by the introduction of Theravada Buddhism from Sri Lanka.

From the eleventh century, the destruction of Buddhism in the Indian mainland by Islamic invasions led to the decline of the Mahayana faith in Southeast Asia. Because continental routes through the Indian subcontinent were compromised, direct sea routes between the Middle East through Sri Lanka and to China developed, leading to the adoption of the

Theravada Buddhism of the Pali Canon, which was introduced to the region around the eleventh century CE from Sri Lanka.

King Anawrahta (1044–1077), the historical founder of the Burmese empire, unified the country and adopted the Theravada Buddhist faith. This initiated the creation of thousands of Buddhist temples at Pagan, the capital, between the eleventh and thirteenth century. Around 2,000 of them are still standing. The power of the Burmese waned with the rise of the Thai and with the seizure of the capital Pagan by the Mongols in 1287, but Theravada Buddhism remained the main Burmese faith to this day.

The Theravada faith was also adopted by the newly founded ethnic Thai kingdom of Sukhothai around 1260. Theravada Buddhism was further reinforced during the Ayutthaya period (fourteenth to eighteenth century), becoming an integral part of the Thai society.

In the continental areas, Theravada Buddhism continued to expand into Laos and Cambodia in the thirteenth century. However, from the fourteenth century, on the coastal fringes and in the islands of Southeast Asia, the influence of Islam proved stronger, expanding into Malaysia, Indonesia, and most of the islands as far as the southern Philippines.

However, since 1966, with Soeharto's rise of power in the aftermath of the bloody events after the so-called "September 30th, 1965 murders," allegedly executed by the Communist Party, there has been a remarkable renaissance of Buddhism in Indonesia. This is partly due to the Soeharto's New Order's requirements for the people of Indonesia to adopt one of the five official religions—Islam, Protestantism, Catholicism, Hinduism, or Buddhism. Today, it is estimated that there are 10 million Buddhists in Indonesia. Many of them are of Chinese ancestry.

NEW SCHOOLS DEVELOP

Tantric Buddhism started as a movement in eastern India around the fifth or the sixth century. Many of the practices of Tantric Buddhism are derived from Brahmanism (the use of mantras, the practice of yoga, and the burning of sacrificial offerings) and have essentially been influenced by Mahayana thought. Tantrism, also called Vajrayana Buddhism, became the dominant form of Buddhism in Tibet in the eighth century.

After the end of the Kushans, Buddhism flourished in India during the dynasty of the Guptas (fourth to sixth century). Mahayana centers of learning were established, especially at Nalanda in northeastern India. It was to become the largest and most influential Buddhist university for many centuries, with famous teachers such as Nagarjuna. The Gupta style of Buddhist art became very influential from Southeast Asia to China as the faith spread there.

Around the year 400 CE, Buddhism had reached as far as Arabia to the west and to Southeast Asia in the east. Mahayana Buddhism had established a major school in what is now Afghanistan, and other teaching centers were located in China, Korea, Mongolia, and Japan.

In fact, during the first few centuries CE, Buddhism made quite an inroad into East Asia. Buddhism probably arrived in China around the first century CE from Central Asia (although there are some traditions about a monk visiting China during Ashoka's reign), and through to the eighth century, it became an extremely active center of Buddhism.

In 475, the Indian monk Bodhidharma traveled to China and established the Cha'an school, which is more commonly known by its Japanese name: Zen. Then, in response, during the first millennium, monks from China made pilgrimages to India to spread the word of Cha'an.

The spread of Buddhism into China also brought with it the Indo-Hellenstic thinking and art that was now expanding in the western region of Asia. There are still Buddhist wall paintings and reliefs in caves, as well as canvas paintings, sculpture, and ritual objects in the area. Eventually, Chinese culture absorbed this newfound art and around the tenth century, most Buddhist art from that area looked more East Asian than Central Asian.

Buddhism flourished during the beginning of the Tang dynasty (618–907). The dynasty was initially characterized by a strong openness to foreign influences, and renewed exchanges with Indian culture due to the numerous travels of Chinese Buddhist monks to India from the fourth to the eleventh century.

However, foreign influences came to be negatively perceived toward the end of the Tang dynasty. In the year 845, the Tang emperor Wu-Tsung outlawed all "foreign" religions in order to support the indigenous Taoism. He had all Buddhist possessions confiscated and destroyed monasteries and temples. Buddhist monks were executed, effectively ending Buddhism's cultural and intellectual dominance in China.

Pure Land and Chan Buddhism, however, continued to prosper for centuries, the latter giving rise to Japanese Zen. In China, Cha'an flourished particularly under the Song dynasty (1127–1279), when its monasteries were great centers of culture and learning.

In Korea, Chinese ambassadors brought scriptures and images around 372 CE, and the country particularly embraced Seon (Korean for Zen) Buddhism from the seventh century onward. However, when the Confucian Yi Dynasty took over in 1392, Buddhism was strongly discriminated against and then almost completely eradicated, except for a remaining Seon movement.

BUDDHISM BECOMES MAINSTREAM

Meanwhile, in Japan (which is the largest Buddhist country today), Buddhism was brought over in the sixth century when monks brought over scriptures and works of art from China. The government adopted Buddhism as its official religion in the seventh century.

Japan was able to preserve many aspects of Buddhism at the very time it was disappearing in India and being suppressed in Central Asia and China because it was at end of the Silk Road and, thus, didn't experience the Islamic and other cultural revolutions.

The creation of Japanese Buddhist art was especially rich between the eighth and thirteenth centuries, during the periods of Nara, Heian, and Kamakura. Starting in 710 CE, numerous temples and monasteries were built in the capital city of Nara, such as the five-story pagoda and Golden Hall of the Horyuji, or the Kofukuji temple. Countless paintings and sculptures were made, often under governmental sponsorship.

From the twelfth and thirteenth centuries, a further development was Zen art, following the introduction of the faith by Dogen and Eisai upon their return from China. Zen art is mainly characterized by original paintings (such as sumi-e and the Enso) and poetry (especially haikus), striving to express the true essence of the world through impressionistic and unadorned "non-dualistic" representations. The search for Enlightenment "in the moment" also led to the development of other important derivative arts, such as the Chanoyu tea ceremony or the Ikebana art of flower arrangement. This evolution went as far as considering almost any human activity as an art with a strong spiritual and esthetic content. First and foremost in those activities were combat techniques (i.e., martial arts).

Buddhism remains very active in Japan to this day. Around 80,000 Buddhist temples are preserved and regularly restored.

Around the year 800, teachers such as Padmasambhava and Atisha brought Vajrayana from India to Tibet. It initially coexisted with the native beliefs in that country at the time, but later Buddhism largely replaced other religions.

Buddhism always remained strong and significant in many areas of India, specifically those parts that border Tibet, Nepal, and Bhutan, even while it was losing ground in Central Asia and Indonesia because of the appearance of Islam. Meanwhile, in China and Japan, Buddhism adapted aspects of Confucianism, Taoism, and Shinto into its understanding. In Tibet, the Vajrayana lineage (now known as Tibetan Buddhism) was preserved even after it disappeared in India.

The influence of Buddhists weakened in the seventh century following the White Hun and Islamic invasions of India, but it was revived under the Pala Empire between the eighth and the twelfth century. The Palas built many temples and created a distinctive school of Buddhist art.

Then, once again, Buddhism hit hard times. In 1193, Turkish Islamic raiders destroyed Nalanda and by the end of the twelfth century, following the Islamic conquest of the remaining Buddhist communities in India, Buddhists mostly disappeared from the country. Hinduism became the primary religion in the region by this time.

Muslims considered Buddhists to be blasphemous, as they believed that the Buddha was more of an idol than a teacher. Thus, they persecuted Buddhists relentlessly, having more tolerance for those whose religion adhered more closely to their own beliefs (such as Christians and Jews.)

EXPANSION OF BUDDHISM TO THE WEST

Over time, Buddhism came to the Western world. To some Westerners, its focus on atheism (i.e., the belief that there is no God and that the world and life is not divinely inspired or created) resonated. For other Westerners, the positive effects of meditation made Buddhism seem like a particularly uplifting religion. Another aspect of Buddhism to which many Westerners responded is its seeming conjunction with modern science, especially physics.

Politically, too, the idea of ahimsa, or non-violence, played a large role in the development of many societies and cultures in the mid to late twentieth century. Mahatma Gandhi and Martin Luther King, Jr., both used this concept to change their cultures and countries. Likewise, the Dalai Lama and Aun San Kyu Yee, both winners of the Nobel Peace Prize, continue their political work as Buddhists. Many poets and novelists found inspiration in Buddhism. The Eightfold Path has even been compared to the twelve steps—the practice used in Alcoholics Anonymous.

Of course, in the West, Buddhism is generally considered exotic and progressive, but in the East, it is traditional and part of the establishment. Buddhist organizations in Asia are well funded and enjoy support from the wealthy and influential. In fact, to some Buddhists, this financial support is considered problematic, as Buddhists are supposed to work to help the poor, not earn money for the temples and sangha.

After the classical encounters between Buddhism and the West recorded in Greco-Buddhist art, there were more meetings of the minds between Europeans and Buddhists in the Middle Ages when the Franciscan friar William of Rubruck traveled to the Mongol court of Mongke in 1253. He did not bring back any reliquaries or texts.

Instead, the major interest in Buddhism emerged during colonial times in the United States, when the study of Asian religions suddenly became fashionable. Still, it wasn't as if anyone in the West converted to Buddhism.

Finally, though, the opening of Japan in 1853 to the Western world created considerable interest for the arts and culture of Japan, and provided access to the most thriving Buddhist culture in the world.

In the latter half of the nineteenth century, Buddhism (along with many other of the world's religions and philosophies) came to the attention of Western intellectuals. These included the German philosopher Schopenhauer and the American philosopher Henry David Thoreau, who translated a Buddhist sutra from French into English.

In 1899, Gordon Douglas became the first Westerner to be ordained as a Buddhist monk. The first Buddhists to arrive in the United States were Chinese. Hired as cheap labor for the railroads and other expanding industries, they established temples in their settlements along the rail lines.

During this same time, spiritual enthusiasts (i.e., ghost seekers and ouija board players) considered almost all Asian religions and traditions to fit into this somewhat mystical sense of religion. Of course, Western Buddhism was hampered at first by poor translations, but soon Western scholars began to translate the texts. For example, in 1879, Sir Edwin Arnold published his poem "The Light of Asia," which told the story of the Buddha in verse.

Then, in 1880, J.R. de Silva and Henry Steel Olcott designed the International Buddhist flag to celebrate the revival of Buddhism in Sri Lanka. Its stripes symbolize universal compassion, the Middle Path, blessings, purity and liberation, wisdom, and the holistic blending of these beliefs. The 1952 World Buddhist Congress accepted the flag as the International Buddhist Flag.

In the mid-1950s, German writer Hermann Hesse showed great interest in Eastern religions and wrote a novel titled *Siddhartha.* In America in the 1950s, beatknik poets and philosophers espoused (with a bit of misunderstanding) the Zen Buddhist philosophy. Dwelling more on the "nothingness" aspect of meditation than the giving spirituality of Buddhism, this laid-back scene went along hand-in-hand with the literary theories of the day.

In the 1960s, many people, including celebrities such as George Harrison (who studied Hinduism), traveled to Asia in pursuit of gurus and ancient wisdom, since they turned their back on the more traditional Christian society. Buddhism had become the fastest-growing religion in Australia and many other Western nations by the 1990s, in contrast with the steady decline of traditional Western beliefs.

TODAY'S BUDDHIST POPULATIONS

Half of the population of East Asia is Buddhist, and almost half of Southeast Asia is. In Europe, the Buddhist population in every area of the continent never goes above 0.3 percent. In all of Europe, the Buddhist population is only 0.42 percent out of a total population of more than 700 million people. In the Americas, the only Buddhist population is found in North America, and even there it is only about 0.5 percent.

The largest Buddhist populations in the world are in China and Japan, although the percentages there are small. The largest Buddhist populations by percentages are in Thailand, Cambodia, Mongolia, and Myanmar, where 94 percent of the populations are Buddhist, and Japan, Bhutan, Sri Lanka, and Vietnam, where 75 percent of the populations are Buddhist.

Worldwide interest in Buddhism, however, far outweighs the number of people who call it their religion. People see movies about the Dalai Lama, attend his speeches, and send money to the Free Tibet campaign. Such interest in Buddhism probably peaked in the late 60s and early 70s, when anti-war sentiments swept the U.S. population. In 2005, the best estimate is that there are 350 million Buddhists in the world.

BUDDHISM COMPARED TO OTHER RELIGIONS

About 75 percent of Americans say they are Christian (of all denominations), and only 0.5 percent of Americans say they practice Buddhism. Here are some of the differences between their beliefs:

Buddhists do not believe in the veracity of either the Old or the New Testament (including The Garden of Eden and the fall of humanity, original sin, and the worldwide flood), a God, the need for a personal savior, the virgin birth, salvation achieved through good works, specific beliefs or sacraments, the power of prayer (as opposed to meditation), eternal life in either heaven or hell, or the resurrection and the return of a savior to earth at some time in the future. Buddhists also don't believe the end of the world will occur.

However, Buddhism, Christianity, and other major world religions share one basic rule of behavior that sums up how to treat others. Two quotations from Buddhist texts that reflect this ethic are, "…a state that is not pleasing or delightful to me, how could I inflict that upon another?" from Samyutta Nikaya v. 353, and "Hurt not others in ways that you yourself would find hurtful," from Udana-Varga 5:18.

These quotations compare closely to Christianity's Golden Rule, from Matthew 7:12: "Therefore all things whatsoever ye would that men should do to you, do ye even so to them," and from the Gospel of Thomas 6, "…and don't do what you hate."

Likewise, almost all religions teach that a person's personality continues after death. In fact, many religious historians indicate that this belief was the prime reason that people were motivated to create religions. Christianity and Buddhism are no exceptions. Never-theless, they conceive of life after death in very different forms: Buddhism teaches that humans are trapped in a repetitive cycle of birth, life, death, and rebirth. One's goal is to escape from this cycle and reach nirvana. In this state of nirvana, the mind experiences complete freedom, liberation, and non-attachment. Suffering ends because desire and craving—the causes of suffering—are no more.

In contrast, Christianity historically has taught that everyone has only a single life on earth. After death, an eternal life awaits everyone, either in Heaven or in Hell. There is no suffering in Heaven; only joy. Suffering is eternal without any hope of cessation for the inhabitants of Hell.

They do share, however, some basic themes of morality, justice, and love. These themes can be found throughout both the Buddha's teaching and the Hebrew and Christian Bible.

Influential Modern Buddhists

From simple questions (e.g., if a tree falls in the wood and no one is there to hear it, does it make a sound?) to profound political statements (e.g., the non-violence of the Reverend Dr. Martin Luther King, Jr.), Buddhism has affected almost all Westerners in ways they often can't quite identify. Westerners can't always remember, for example, that it was a Buddhist who set himself on fire during the Vietnam War, but they do remember his image and the way it reverberated around the world. Today, years later, thousands of Westerners put "Free Tibet" bumper stickers on their cars to rally around the Dalai Lama, who has become a bestselling author in the United States and throughout Europe.

Although few Westerners follow the Eightfold Path or seek refuge in the Three Baskets (see Becoming a Buddhist), millions of them reap the benefits of meditation and see solutions to their problems in programs that rely on clear thinking. In addition, they read the works, see the films, and admire the sports psychologies of numerous Buddhists, including Martin Scorsese, Richard Gere, Phil Jackson, Michael Stipe, Allan Ginsburg, and Lisa Simpson.

D. T. Suzuki

D. T. Suzuki authored many books and essays on Buddhism and Zen that were instrumental in spreading interest in Zen to the West. Suzuki grew up poor with his mother, and he used to look for answers about his situation in life by studying various religions. He began to study spirituality under Kosen Roshi and continued with Soyen Shaku. Both of his teachers felt that he was exceptional, and under Soyen Shaku, his practice became focused on internal and non-verbal meditations and knowledge, including long periods of practicing zazen. He described this experience in his book *The Training of the Zen Buddhist Monk.*

Suzuki gained a working knowledge of Chinese, Sanskrit, Pali, and several European languages in order to further his religious studies. In 1893, Suzuki accompanied Shaku to the World Parliament of Religions in Chicago. When a scholar asked Shaku to help translate some Asian spiritual literature, Shaku recommended Suzuki for the position. Soon after, Suzuki moved to Chicago and helped translate the classic Tao Te Ching from ancient Chinese into English. Meanwhile, Suzuki began to write Outlines of Mahayana Buddhism.

After marrying Beatrice Erskine Lane, a Theosophist and Radcliffe graduate, Suzuki moved with her to Japan. The two dedicated themselves to teaching Mahayana Buddhism throughout the world, and together they founded the Eastern Buddhist Society. Suzuki wrote some of Western society's most celebrated examinations of Buddhism, particularly its Zen school. He eventually became a professor at Columbia University. His Introduction to Zen Buddhism was published with a thirty-page commentary written by Carl Jung.

Suzuki once wrote, "We say, 'In calmness there should be activity; in activity there should be calmness.' Actually, they are the same thing; to say 'calmness' or to say 'activity' is just to express different interpretations of one fact. There is harmony in our activity, and where there is harmony there is calmness."

The Dalai Lama, or Kundun

Tenzin Gyatso, who was born to a peasant family in a small Tibetan village, was recognized as His Holiness the Fourteenth Dalai Lama at the age of two. He is the spiritual and temporal (i.e., physical) leader of both the Tibetan people and Tibetan Buddhists. He is the reincarnation of his predecessor the Thirteenth Dalai Lama.

Each Dalai Lama, which means "Ocean of Wisdom," is the manifestation of the Bodhisattva of Compassion, who chose to reincarnate to serve the people. Tibetans call the Dalai Lama Yeshin Norbu, the Wish-fulfilling Gem, or, simply, Kundun, meaning The Presence.

Kundun received the Geshe Lharampa Degree (i.e., Doctorate of Buddhist Philosophy) after the preliminary examinations at each of the three monastic universities: Drepung, Sera, and Ganden in Tibet. The final examination was held in Lhasa during the annual Monlam Festival of Prayer. In the morning, he was questioned on logic by thirty scholars. In the afternoon, he debated fifteen scholars on the Middle Path. In the evening, thirty-five scholars tested his wisdom of the canon of monastic discipline and the study of metaphysics. His Holiness passed the examinations with honors before a large audience of monk scholars.

In 1950, at age sixteen, The Dalai Lama assumed full political power as Head of State and Government when China began to threaten to take over Tibet. In 1954, he went to Beijing to attempt negotiations with Mao Tse-Tung and other Chinese leaders, including Chou En-Lai and Deng Xiaoping. Then, in 1956, while visiting India to attend the 2500th Buddha Jayanti, he met with Prime Minister Nehru and Premier Chou about what appeared to be beginning of the end of a free Tibet. In 1959, after a brutal Chinese military occupation of Tibet, he fled to Dharamsala, India. Dharamsala is now known as "Little Lhasa" because it is the official seat of the Tibetan Government-in-Exile.

Because of Kundun's intense but soft-spoken political lobbying, the General Assembly of the United Nations has adopted three resolutions calling for China to leave Tibet. He also has guaranteed that the future government of Tibet, previously a theocracy, will be a democracy. "I always believe that it is much better to have a variety of religions, a variety of philosophies, rather than one single religion or philosophy. This is necessary because of the different mental dispositions of each human being. Each religion has certain unique ideas or techniques, and learning about them can only enrich one's own faith."

While in exile, The Dalai Lama has set up educational, cultural, and religious institutions that have brought Tibetan Buddhism to people throughout the world. At the Congressional Human Rights Caucus in 1987, he proposed a Five-Point Peace Plan that calls for the designation of Tibet as a zone of peace, an end to the massive transfer of ethnic Chinese into Tibet, restoration of fundamental human rights and democratic freedoms, and the abandonment of China's use of Tibet for nuclear weapons production and the dumping of nuclear waste. He also urged "earnest negotiations" on the future of Tibet and relations between the Tibetan and Chinese people. There has, however, been little movement on this issue by the Chinese government.

When he won The Nobel Peace Prize in 1990, he said, "The need for simple human-to-human relation-ships is becoming increasingly urgent…Today the world is smaller and more interdependent. One nation's problems can no longer be solved by itself completely. Thus, without a sense of universal responsibility, our very survival becomes threatened. Basically, universal responsibility is feeling for other people's suffering just as we feel our own. It is the realization that even our enemy is entirely motivated by the quest for happiness. We must recognize that all beings want the same thing that we want. This is the way to achieve a true understanding, unfettered by artificial consideration."

Many Buddhists believe that to be ordained by a higher order monk will bring about positive karma, so they travel as many miles as necessary to be ordained into the sangha by the Dalai Lama, even if they do not intend to be monks or nuns in this life.

Allan Ginsberg, Jack Kerouac, and the Dharma Bums

Written in 1958 as the follow-up to *On the Road, The Dharma Bums* is Jack Kerouac's novel about a group of writers flirting with and flying high on Buddhism. As in *On the Road*, Kerouac turned his group of friends into a barely disguised cast of characters. For example, Japhy Ryder in Dharma Bums is the equivalent of Dean Moriarty in On The Road—they are both inspired by Neal Cassady.

Kerouac's free-style poetic approach to storytelling reflects his and his friends' spiritual influences and interests:

> "But now I was three miles into the industrial jungle of L.A. in mad sick sniffling smog night and had to sleep all that night by a wire fence in a ditch by the tracks being waked up all night by rackets of Southern Pacific and Santa Fe switchers bellyaching around, till fog and clear of midnight when I breathed better (thinking and praying in my sack) but then more fog and smog again and horrible damp white cloud of dawn and my bag too hot to sleep in and outside too raw to stand, nothing but

horror all night long, except at dawn a little bird
blessed me."

Kerouac died relatively young, as did Neal Cassady,
his hero and inspiration, but Allan Ginsburg, the genius
Beat poet, lived long and well, studying Buddhism,
writing, and teaching. His poem, "Sunflower Sutra," is
a celebration of life. Here is one stanza:

> "We're not our skin of grime, we're not our dread
> bleak dusty imageless locomotive, we're all golden
> sunflowers inside, blessed by our own seed & hairy
> naked accomplishment-bodies growing into mad
> black formal sunflowers in the sunset, spied on by our
> eyes under the shadow of the mad locomotive river-
> bank sunset Frisco hilly tincan evening sitdown vision."

In 1974, Ginsberg and Anne Waldman started the
Jack Kerouac School of Disembodied Poetics at Naropa
Institute (now Naropa University) in Boulder, CO. The
school was founded by Chogyam Trungpa Rinpoche and
modeled after Nalanda University, a Buddhist learning
center that existed between the fifth and eleventh
centuries in India. At Naropa, instruction is given in the
arts, psychology, religious studies, and other fields, using
a Buddhist practice as its basis.

Allan Watts

Alan Watts was a writer and philosopher who was
instrumental in bringing Buddhism to California and
the literary world. He lived from 1916 to 1973 and wrote

more than twenty books on comparative religion (specifically on Zen Buddhism). Because they were very free form and poetic, his speaking engagements and writings influenced the Beatniks, but really he was the link between Suzuki's teachings and the acceptance of Buddhism in the 1950s and on words.

His books featured essays on philosophical topics that had never before been addressed in the West, such as personal identity, the true nature of reality, and the pursuit of happiness. He also excelled at relating his scientific knowledge to the teachings of Eastern religions and philosophies. Eventually, however, people responded to his touchy-feely approach rather than to his ability to explain esoteric Eastern terms in poetic imagery, which paved the way for books such as *Zen and The Art of Motorcycle Maintenance*. His book, *The Way of Zen*, is a classic for all Zen students.

Here is a sample of his writing: "The difficulty for most of us in the modern world is that the old-fashioned idea of God has become incredible or implausible. When we look through our telescopes and microscopes, or when we just look at nature, we have a problem. Somehow the idea of God we get from the holy scriptures doesn't seem to fit the world around us, just as you wouldn't ascribe a composition by Stravinsky to Bach. The style of God venerated in the church, mosque, or synagogue seems completely different from the style of the natural universe. It's hard to conceive of the author of one as the author of the other."

Pema Chodron

Pema Chodron is a Tibetan Buddhist nun and leading meditation teacher for Western audiences. She was not born into this life but rather adopted it.

Ane Pema Chodron was born Deirdre Blomfield-Brown in 1936, attended Miss Porter's School in Connecticut, and graduated from the University of California at Berkeley. In her mid-thirties, Pema met Lama Chime Rinpoche. She became a novice nun in 1974 and was ordained by His Holiness the Sixteenth Karmapa.

Ane Pema served as the director of Karma Dzong in Boulder, Colorodo, until 1984, when she moved to rural Cape Breton, Nova Scotia, to be the director of Gampo Abbey. Her first two books, *The Wisdom of No Escape* and *Start Where You Are*, were wildly successful, and she became a Buddhist celebrity.

Her books are now best sellers, even among non-Buddhists. Her most recent books are *When Things Fall Apart* and *The Places That Scare You*, which seemed particularly relevant after the events of September 2001. She continues to run the Gampo Abbey, which is the first Tibetan monastery for Westerners.

Thich Nhat Hanh

Many Westerners were first exposed to Buddhism during the Vietnam War, when Buddhist monks set themselves on fire (called self-immolation) and their deaths were shown on television. The monks did so to protest the government's refusal to allow a celebration of Vesak, a Buddhist holiday—not to protest the war. This was significant not just because of its drama, but because it showed the world what Buddhists are willing to give up (i.e., their own lives) for what they believe is right. Unlike the rest of the world, the Buddhist monks did not hurt others; they only hurt themselves.

This protest was also significant because it was political, not religious.

Thich Nhat Hanh, a Vietnamese Buddhist monk, coined the phrased "engaged Buddhism" to describe those Buddhists who seek social change within the paradigm of their Buddhist practice. Thich Nhat Hanh left Vietnam in 1966 and relocated. He is the author of numerous books and speaks around the world about the influence that meditation and calm abiding can have on others.

One issue for Buddhists around this kind of political activity is realizing that the main purpose isn't about one political party winning or one agenda coming out on top. In fact, no one is seen as the enemy or in the wrong. The enemy is never a person, but a frame of mind—one polluted by greed, anger, or ignorance.

Thich Quang Duc

Westerners were horrified by and yet admiring of a Vietnamese Buddhist monk who set himself on fire at a busy intersection in Saigon in the early 1960s. The act was televised around the world, and one reporter wrote:

"Flames were coming from a human being; his

body was slowly withering and shriveling up, his head blackening and charring. In the air was the smell of burning human flesh; human beings burn surprisingly quickly. Behind me I could hear the sobbing of the Vietnamese who were now gathering. I was too shocked to cry, too confused to take notes or ask questions, too bewildered to even think…As he burned he never moved a muscle, never uttered a sound, his outward composure in sharp contrast to the wailing people around him."

That monk, Thich Quang Duc, was protesting the administration of the Vietnamese Prime Minister Ngo Dinh Diem, who was Catholic and who was suppressing Buddhism in that highly Buddhist country. The monastery to which this monk belonged was thus made famous, and the car in which he drove himself to Saigon is there, along with a picture of his self-immolation. Members of his sangha attempted to cremate his heart after his death, but it wouldn't burn. It is now a holy relic in the Reserve Bank of Vietnam.

It is said that the first lady of Vietnam at the time responded to this act of protest by saying that she would "clap hands at seeing another monk barbecue show."

The Rinpoches

Rinpoche is Tibetan for Precious One, and the name has been given to members of numerous lines of royal Tibetan Buddhist teachers, including the Shambhala lineage, Kagyu lineage, and Nyingma lineage. Many of these teachers have become familiar to Western Buddhists. They include Chogyam Trungpa Rinpoche and Sogyal Rinpoche, who wrote The Tibetan Book of Living and Dying, and Gehlek Rinpoche.

Chogyam Trungpa Rinpoche was one of the most outstanding Tibetan Vajrayana Masters to teach in the West. He started the Shambhala schools of meditation, Naropa Institute, and wrote various discourses on Buddhism for Westerners.

Meanwhile, The Tibetan Book of Living and Dying is an influential work of spiritual significance because it focuses on the positive aspects and reality of death. The positive aspect is that if you face and embrace the reality of death then you will be able to celebrate life.

Its author said, "Perhaps the deepest reason why we are afraid of death is because we do not know who we are. We believe in a personal, unique, and separate identity; but if we dare to examine it, we find that this identity depends entirely on an endless collection of things to prop it up: our name, our 'biography,' our partners, family, home, job, friends, credit cards…It is on their fragile and transient support that we rely for our security. So when they are all taken away, will we have any idea of who we really are?

Without our familiar props, we are faced with just ourselves, a person who we do not know, an unnerving stranger with whom we have been living all the time but we never really wanted to meet. Isn't that why we have tried to fill every moment of time with noise and activity, however boring or trivial, to ensure that we are never left in silence with this stranger on our own?"

Gehlek Rinpoche founded The Jewel Heart Organization in the United States and has a large following in The Netherlands. He was born in Lhasa, Tibet, and is an incarnate Lama of Drepung Monastic University, the largest Tibetan monastery that ever existed, housing at its zenith more than 13,000 monks.

Aung San Suu Kyi

Aung San Suu Kyi is the daughter of the Burmese general who negotiated that country's independence from Britain and who was later assassinated. She has long been held as a political prisoner by the Myanmar (Burma's name was changed to Myanmar after its liberation from England) government. She is a nonviolent pro-democracy activist who has won the Sakharov Prize for Freedom of Thought and the Nobel Peace Prize. She used the Nobel Peace Prize's $1.3 million prize money to establish a health and education trust for the Burmese people.

After studying at Oxford and at the University of London, Suu Kyi returned to Myanmar in 1988 to care for her ailing mother. Just then, a new military junta took power in her country after students demanding democracy staged mass demonstrations. Heavily influenced by Gandhi's nonviolence, Aung San Suu Kyi entered politics to work for democratization and was placed under house arrest in 1989. She was offered freedom if she would leave the country, but she refused.

The military junta held elections in 1990 and the "National League for Democracy" won, which meant that she was supposed to be named Prime Minister. However, the military refused to hand over power.

Her husband and children remained in the United Kingdom during her house arrest and, despite being released in July 1995, she never returned to the West, because the Myanmar government made it clear that she would not be allowed back into her country. When her husband, Michael Aris, was diagnosed with cancer, the government would not allow him into Myanmar. Aung wouldn't leave. She never saw him before his death.

In September 2000, she was again placed under house arrest. In 2002, she was released, and the government said she was free to move, which she seemed to believe. However, at the end of May 2003, she was again placed under house arrest, where she remains today.

Richard Gere

Few movie audiences realize that actor Richard Gere is embarking on a spiritual journey in his personal life. He began to read about Tibetan Buddhism while in his early 20s to conquer the profound sadness he felt. He began to study Zen Buddhism while living in Los Angeles and then met the Dalai Lama. Gere tells the story best:

"I had been a Zen student for five or six years before I met His Holiness in India. We started out with a little small talk and then he said, 'Oh, so you're an actor?' He thought about that a second, and then he said, 'So when you do this acting and you're angry, are you really angry? When you're acting sad, are you really sad? When you cry, are you really crying?' I gave him some kind of actor answer, like it was more effective if you really believed in the emotion that you were portraying. He looked very deeply into my eyes and just started laughing. Hysterically. He was laughing at the idea that I would believe emotions are real, that I would work very hard to believe in anger and hatred and sadness and pain and suffering."

He has said that the meeting changed his life, and he has traveled to India, where the Dalai Lama lives, to study with him and other teachers. He works actively to free Tibet from Chinese rule, and he has sponsored many talks and events in the United States that feature the Dalai Lama and foster his teaching.

He has said about Tibet, "I am convinced that [the institutions of] the great dharma were designed to create good-hearted people; everything in the society was there to feed it. That became decadent—there were bad periods, there were good periods, whatever. But the gist of the society was to create good-hearted people, bodhisattvas, to create a very strong environment where people could achieve Enlightenment. Imagine that in America! I mean, we have no structure for Enlightenment. We have a very strong Christian heritage and Jewish heritage, one of compassion, one of altruism. Good people. But we have very little that encourages Enlightenment—total liberation."

Phil Jackson and *Sacred Hoops*

When the Chicago Bulls and the Los Angeles Lakers became two of the dominant basketball teams around the turn of the twenty-first century, many credited Phil Jackson, the teams' coach, for its success. And Jackson, the author of *Sacred Hoops*, is a coach like no other.

His parents were fundamental Christian ministers, so Jackson grew up in a simple home with a faith-based center. As a player and, later, as a coach, Jackson developed an interest in Zen Buddhism and began a regular meditation practice.

"'Living in the moment' is something that I will continue to always understand and associate with my life. It sounds like a minor thing, but it's very big when you're playing at this level to really be aware of everything around you."

Jackson uses other religions and philosophies to infuse his coaching, but it is his cool head and calm spirit that that brought attention from players, fans, and the media. Jackson didn't stress competitiveness with the other team but with the self. He offered wisdom so that aggression was eased on the court and self-mastery was encouraged. He was clearly cited as one of the first figures to bring Eastern philosophy to Western sports. Eventually yoga practice, meditation, and mindfulness training became as much a part of athleticism as the actual practice of the sport.

Buddhism
and Psychology

The development of the psychological, psychiatric, and emotional health fields of study over the past 150 years in the Western world has occurred just as Buddhism was also arriving from the East. Many therapists and religious scholars have commented and written on the similarities between the religion and the science.

First, they both begin with a state of disease within a person. This sense of unhappiness or dread leads a person to seek a relief from an unnamed unhappiness or feeling within them. Second, the person goes to a therapist (or, in the case of Buddhism, a guru, lama, or teacher) to help them seek the happiness that lies within them. Finally, much of what is worked on and improved upon is the patient or seeker's own mind-chatter or ignorance (about the self, not in the intellectual sense).

Even therapists and physicians who don't turn to Buddhism in any way often rely on techniques such as meditation and yoga to encourage their patients to relax and think more clearly and happily.

One of the most well known Buddhist psychologists and yoga teachers is Stephen Cope, who works and practices at Kripalu, a well-known school in Massachusetts. He has written the following: "Early on in the transmission of the Eastern contemplative techniques to the West, Carl Jung warned that we should not take on these practices. He believed that they would too severely deconstruct the Western psyche. He warned that we should look instead to our own traditions, our own spiritual and psychological sources. Our experience over the last twenty-five years has shown us that Jung was clearly wrong for the most part. But he was right about one thing: We will need to find our own idiosyncratic paths into these traditions. We will have to make them ours. We will have to bring the principles alive with the stories of real Americans practice—the peculiar enigmas and conflicts of our twenty-first-century lives. We will need to respect our own cultures, psyches, and styles." (from *Will Yoga & Meditation Really Change My Life?*, Kripalu, 2003).

NOT WHY BUT HOW

On the day after Christmas in 2004, a tsunami ravaged the countries surrounding the Indian Ocean, killing more than 150,000 people and devastating the lives of millions more. A headline in The New York Times—and in magazines—said "Where was God?" Callers to radio shows wondered, "Why did God let this happen?" Buddhists do not ask questions like these; instead, they ask questions such as "How do I deal with this event?" Buddhists strive to accept reality as it is while, at the same time, turning to religion for guidance on how to live in a way that helps all human beings, as well as animals and the planets.

For Buddhists, it is our attachment to the world looking a certain way that makes us feel sad about an event. Of course, we are attached to our children or our family and friends, so if they die, we are sad and scared. But believing that it is punishment or that it is bad without a possibility for good is our own limitation.

Buddhists also do not believe in a divine entity. Thus, no God caused or allowed a tsunami or any other event.

Buddhism and the Twelve Steps

In the middle of the twentieth century, Americans (and then people of other nationalities) began to see their dependence on alcohol and other drugs as more of a problem than a solution to their problems. Alcoholics Anonymous was founded by Bill W. and a friend when, together, they offered each other support and a framework to overcome their intense alcohol addictions. This framework was called The Twelve Steps.

The Twelve Steps were later adapted to work for overeating, drug addiction, sex addiction, and other dysfunctional ways to think and behave. The men who created the program were Christians, and the Twelve Steps were and are geared to those who believed in one

God (although some of the language has been changed to accommodate people of all faiths, even non-believers).

Meanwhile, over the years, Buddhists and Twelve Steppers have noticed and commented on the similarity between the Steps and the Eightfold Path. Like the Eightfold Path, Twelve Step programs are about recovery from the inner darkness within a person's soul. This emptiness may manifest itself as alcoholism, drug addiction, compulsive overeating, or gambling.

There are Twelve Step meetings and programs all over the world, and some of them are geared directly to Buddhists who "work the program."

These are The Buddhist Twelve Steps:

- We admitted that by ourselves we were powerless to overcome our own fundamental darkness and live what we truly believe.

- We are open to leaving our self-imposed isolation and to raise our life condition. We release the delusion that we are alone or unsupported in an indifferent, or hostile, world. We come to believe "we are many in body and one in spirit."

- We vow to allow our true self to manifest. This is a determination that aligns our lives with the rhythm of the living cosmos, or Mystic Law.

- This inventory must be as honest as we can be at this time. We must include our good, or bad, thoughts and actions. As Buddhists we know good and evil are two, but not two. Can we be as thorough in listing our basic goodness as the times we have been angry, full of self-pity, guilty, resentful, or spiteful?

- We no longer blame people, places and things for our lack of progress. By admitting our defects to another being, we are admitting our interdependence. It was our denial of our interdependence that led to our original dysfunction.

- We are entirely ready to let your true self reassert itself in the world.

- As we allow our true nature to emerge, our thoughts and actions change.

- Changing the poison of our past into medicine for today. This step is a reflective step showing ourselves the effects of our disease and denial on others. We can no longer say that we did not hurt anyone except ourselves. We are preparing to change our karma. We become responsible for our own spiritual evolution.

- Although we may feel powerless when making amends, we discover that we've always had the real power to change for the better and wake up. By seizing the moment and making amends, we are ensuring that our disease becomes fully integrated into the whole, real human being we are becoming. We embrace the world and the universe itself by recovering our true nature, which was betrayed by our denial. The only amend that the universe will accept is your consent to become a real human being and resume your correct job of being attentive to this moment.

- Anything that drains our hope and life force limits what we think is possible. Living with Awareness. Honest awareness is key.

- Twelve Step programs grants us the freedom to discover our own meaningful definitions, ones that will work for us. If our Higher Power is present and implicit in each moment, then we can gain conscious contact by becoming aware of our place in the universe.

- This is the bodhisattva step in recovery. We came into this life to share our recovery, our awakening, our Enlightenment. As we attain a way of life that is in agreement with the deepest dictates of our being, we know joy.

Buddhism and Modern Science

More than 2,500 years ago, the Buddha and Buddhists discussed pratitya-samutpada, the concept that the world is not made up of solids but is really a series of endless interlocked events, energy, and perceptions that have no reality aside from what is perceived by people and animals.

This would seem to disagree with classic physics, which postulates that the material world is independent of, and unrelated to, the human mind. Its existence is considered as an objective reality and undeniable fact. This was true of mountains and atoms. Size didn't matter.

However, scientists found that although electrons

used to appear to be objectively real, in fact, an electron's energy will immediately be dissipated by the attractive force of the nucleus forcing the electron to crash into it within a moment. Therefore, given the classic model of electrons, atoms could not maintain their existence more than a moment. This threw off the traditional concept of particle science as the basic component of reality. With this new understanding, Einstein and others developed quantum physics.

According to this new scientific thinking, an electron cannot exist until it is actually observed, so before it is observed, it exists in "pre-existence." This condition creates innumerable possibilities and probabilities because the electron then exactly exists with "potential," not with "reality."

An act of observation, dependent upon location and relationship, will isolate an electron, and its existence will become real.

Isn't this, in some ways, related to a Buddhist's perception of the mind and thoughts? Because elementary particles are the basic building blocks of the material (and biological) universe, this means that even the material universe cannot exist without observation. This universe, according to quantum physics, is dependent on the human mind, and observation must determine not only the way of existence of the present or future universe, but also the past universe.

Meanwhile, medical science has only proven the efficacy of Buddhist thinking and formulation. For example, it has been proven that meditation can reduce the symptoms of stress-related illnesses and improve the heart health of those who practice it, no matter what their religious beliefs.

In fact, in the 1970s, medical researchers found that meditation actually produces a fourth state of consciousness, one that they hadn't previously known existed (the other three of which include being awake, being asleep, and dreaming). Researchers actually used, as their definition of this state, the ancient Vedic (i.e., Hindu) texts: consistent, silent, uninvolved inner awareness that was measured as increased alpha waves in the frontal lobes.

Meditation doesn't only help you achieve a blissful state when you're on the cushion. It takes awhile to learn this, according to researchers at the Maharishi University of Management in Fairfield, IO—anywhere from seven to thirty years—but eventually, after dedicated practice, people can maintain the calm state of mind even when they stop actually meditating.

The physician most responsible for bringing this research to the public (and the medical establishment) is Jon Kabat-Zinn, who founded the Center for Mindfulness at the University of Massachusetts Medical School. His programs have been used in and adapted to health education programs throughout the United States, changing the way patients with all types of illnesses, including cancer and heart disease, handle their illnesses. Even the title of one of his books, *Wherever you Go, There You Are*, has become a modern-day mantra.

Taking Refuge,
or Becoming a Buddhist

Many people these days learn about Buddhism through yoga practice or through hearing about the Dalai Lama and other important world leaders. The teachings appeal to them, but there are few places to go for them in the Western World.

The Buddha taught that the aim of a Buddhist practice is to become free of dukkah, or suffering, but even amid all of his specific teachings, there is still confusion about how to accomplish this. To some Buddhists, this means awakening to the realization of anatman (egolessness, or the absence of a permanent or substantial self). Other Buddhist scriptures encourage the practitioner to cleanse himself or herself of the mental and moral defilements of the "worldly self" and thereby penetrate through to the "Buddha-nature" within. This is sometimes called the "true self," and when a person reaches it, he or she is transformed into a buddha. Some other schools appeal to bodhisattvas for a favorable rebirth, while others say you don't have to do any of these things.

Most, if not all, Buddhist schools teach a minimum to their followers: think clearly, perform good and wholesome deeds, and avoid bad and harmful acts. Basic Buddhist morality teaches harmlessness and moderation, and the mental training concentrates on moral discipline (sila), meditative concentration (samadhi), and wisdom (prana).

As in other systems of belief, people may think of themselves as Buddhist having been born into a family of Buddhists, or into a culture where Buddhism is predominant, and may never actually go through any ritual. However, Buddhists do not have to give up their other religious affiliation to practice Buddhism (although some religions ask Buddhists to do things that go against their principles, so a Buddhist will have to choose). Buddhists also don't have to change the way they eat, dress, or pray, although many people choose to do so. As one Rinpoche said, "Just because you make a new friend, you don't have to give up your old friend."

THE CEREMONY

More formally, however, one can complete the ritual called Taking Refuge, which symbolizes becoming a truly committed Buddhist and one that is part of the sangha. To prepare for taking refuge, a person will traditionally bathe to symbolically wash away the past. This creates a feeling of purification and rebirth. Although no one is required to dress a certain way (aside from appearing modest), many Asian cultures associate yellow with religious vows and red with special occasions, so those colors are common among Buddhists.

Then, in the presence of someone from the sangha (specifically, in front of an ordained Buddhist teacher, priest, monk, or nun), the person asks for permission to join the sangha. Usually the group stands in front of a shrine with elements that represent the Three Jewels, such as a statue of Buddha; offerings of food, flowers, bowls of water, and incense; and an offering of light (usually a lit candle).

The teacher will explain that there are prerequisites to becoming a Buddhist: 1) you understand what you are doing; 2) you come of your own free will; and 3) you promise to observe the precept to not take any life intentionally.

The person desiring Refuge then kneels on the right knee with his or her palms joined below the chin. This pose is called anjali. Then the person states the following three times: "I, (with your full name), request refuge." On the third time, the person's name will have changed, which symbolizes entering the stream. Now you repeat your request with your new name. In Mahayana Buddhism, the bodhisattva vow is incorporated in the refuge vow: From now until the time of Enlightenment, I take refuge in the Buddha, the dharma and the sangha, for the benefit of all mother-beings.

The monk or lama then asks the person to approach and cuts a tiny lock of hair from the crown of his or her head. This is a reminder that the person is leaving the past behind and symbolically experiencing her own death. The "new" person offers thanks. The new member of the sangha offers the lama a thin white silk (or rayon) scarf called a katta, which is used in the Tibetan cultures as an offering. The teacher often returns this gift by placing it around the offerer's shoulders as a form of blessing.

A Buddhist can take refuge more than once, and sometimes people renew their commitment.

Not everyone has access to a guru, lama, or teacher, so it is possible to enter the stream with actually having a sangha around you. Buddhists tell such people to take Refuge before a book of Buddhist Sutras and an image of the Buddha Shakyamuni.

The Future Buddha

In Buddhism, Maitreya is the future Buddha, a bodhisattva who will eventually appear on earth, achieve complete Enlightenment, and teach the dharma. Maitreya is comparable to the second coming in other religions, such as Kali, the final avatar of Vishnu in Hinduism, and Jesus in Christianity.

Maitreya is typically depicted sitting on an altar with both feet on the ground, which symbolizes that he has not yet ascended his throne. Maitreya's name come from the word "maitri," which means universal love in Sanskrit. Buddhist teachings say that when the Buddha's teachings disappear from this world, negativity and misfortune will grow until, spontaneously moved by his overwhelming compassion, Maitreya will manifest in our world as a radiantly beautiful spiritual teacher, inspiring people to practice the path of virtue, especially loving-kindness.

"I GREW UP IN A VERY URBAN, NOISY BROOKLYN, AND HAVE ALWAYS BEEN INTRIGUED BY SILENCE. AT FIRST I WANTED EXTERNAL SILENCE, BUT THAT GOAL SOON BECAME INTERNAL SILENCE. IT'S A VAST REALM. PEOPLE HAVE SAID SPACE, OR THE OCEAN, IS THE 'LAST FRONTIER' BUT I THINK THERE'S ANOTHER FRONTIER—EACH OF US IS AN ENTIRE UNIVERSE TO BE EXPLORED. ENJOYING THE QUALITY OF STILLNESS AND JOY THAT COMES UP IN PRACTICE, BEING WITH WHATEVER IS THERE, IS JUST WONDERFUL."

—Larry Rosenburg

I actually became somewhat disillusioned with Buddhism as I wrote this book—because I did as the Buddha instructed and measured his teachings and the dharma again my own experience and perceptions. The mythology of the Buddha's biography took away from the intensity of his teachings and the usefulness of the Eightfold Path in my mind. Also, Buddhism's unwavering faith in reincarnation seemed over the top.

But a funny thing happened as I continued to write. While listening to National Public Radio one day, I heard the end of a report on reincarnation and Buddhism. The reporter had asked the Dalai Lama what Buddhists would do if reincarnation were found to be absolutely false.

"We would go on," The Dalai Lama replied.

I understood what he meant and was completely reassured.

What the Dalai Lama meant, I believe, is that reincarnation—or the release from samsara—is not what matters most to today's Buddhists. Rather, it is the practice that matters, the day-to-day living with the Eightfold Path.

No matter what my opinion on the Buddha's mystical birth or his various incarnations, my doubts never took away from one personal truth: Practicing Buddhism has brought me a peace of mind and a workable philosophy for many years. In much the same way that Christians of this day and age ask themselves

"What Would Jesus Do?" I seek wisdom in my life
by asking myself not what the Buddha would do,
but instead, "What is The Buddhist thing to do?"

Thus, when anything happens to me, I try to
respond with love, compassion, and kindness. I am not
always successful with this, I admit. I am a woman
who loves, for example, to gossip and talk about people.
To me, this kind of talk isn't just not harmful, it can
be both entertaining and a bonding experience. In fact,
I once interviewed a psychologist who told me that two
people feel closest when they are talking about—and
agreeing upon—their opinions of a third person.

Then, one day, I was listening to someone else talk
behind the back of another person. And the first person
sounded petty and mean to me, not entertaining.
I reflected upon this and realized that this was how I
sounded to others—catty, backhanded, and untrust-
worthy.

I actually called a yoga teacher I know, someone
who is a committed Buddhist, and told her how I was
feeling. She answered me with great compassion and
wisdom saying, "The most important thing is that you
are feeling unhappy about your behavior. It is hurting
your soul, not necessarily others. It is because of what
you feel inside that change will come. This awareness is
what will move you on your path."

This was particularly wise, to me, because she
didn't invoke a Ten Commandments-like teaching that
might say, essentially, "You are wrong and you will pay."
Nor did she talk about how I was hurting others.

My teacher was trying to tell me that wisdom comes from the desire to be better. To love ourselves. To take care of ourselves. We cannot seek to be kind to others—one of the great and most important teachings of Buddhism—if we aren't kind to ourselves.

I believe that we are put on this earth to follow our own great spiritual paths. When I see people acting out of avarice or anger, the pain I feel is not for their victims, but for the individual they are hurting most—themselves.

Because Buddhism asks you to be a good person for the sake of your own personal growth (to use a particularly Western phrase), I believe that, in turn, it creates kinder and more loving people. And then, ultimately, the world as a whole will be kinder and more loving.

That is, of course, one purpose of religion.

Likewise, I believe that many of us turn to religion when we are in a particular crisis—we have lost a job or a loved one, become scared for our safety or healthy—and so we ask God to help us. To save us.

What I appreciate about Buddhism is that it puts the will of God into our own hands. We do not ask Buddha or God to change reality for us. Instead, as Buddhists, we strive to see reality clearly, accept it, and deal with it in a way that is loving and kind, as well as wise. We do not look out for our own greed or ego, but instead we try to act kindly and lovingly for the greater good, which includes our own health and happiness.

Ahimsa — (Sanskrit) Non-violence or non-harming. This is a central idea of Buddhism and for many Buddhists it includes vegetarianism.

Anatman — (Sanskrit) Non-self. Buddhists do not believe there is a self within the body, as in an unchanging soul, spirit, or personality that exists throughout one lifetime or many lifetimes. Instead, we mistake our sensations for a soul. Pali: anatta.

Anitya — (Sanskrit) Impermanence. Everything is transient, according to Buddhists.

Arhant — (Sanskrit) Worthy One. Someone who has become a buddha. Pali: arahant.

Asceticism — An extreme form of self-denial, usually meaning fasting, celibacy, and, to some, true suffering in terms of self-flagellation and exhausting pilgrimages.

Bodhisattva — (Sanskrit) A person striving to reach nirvana and become the next buddha by exhibiting compassion and commitment to help others reach nirvana. Pali: bodhisatta.

Brahman — The ultimate reality, according to Hinduism. Not to be confused with Brahmin, a social caste.

Buddha — To awaken. There is more than one buddha, but the Buddha is known as that because of his teaching and development of a sangha. "Buddha" is derived from a word in the Sanskrit verbal root "budh," meaning "to awaken or be Enlightened."

Buddha nature—The ability within every person to awaken and achieve Enlightenment.

Calm abiding—A form of meditation that features serenity and awareness with no judgment. In Sanskrit: samatha.

Caste—Indian society both before and after the Buddha had castes or varnas, which were believed to reflect a person's past life. Because of that, it was almost impossible to change castes in a lifetime according to Hindu society. It was against this caste system that many Buddhists adopted their views of reincarnation, believing that good deeds and not the caste you were born into could help to alter your spiritual path.

Deva—A spiritual being (without a body) who inhabits the spiritual world but is still subject to rebirth.

Dhammapada—A book of the Buddha's teachings.

Dharma—(Sanskrit) Buddhist teachings. Pali: dhamma.

Dukkha—Suffering, dissatisfaction, stress.

Enlightenment—The release from samsara. The translation of nirvana. An indescribable state of freedom and bliss.

Insight meditation—A meditation in which you strive to see life as it is. See vipassana.

Jainism—A religion in India at the time of Buddha. Its founder, Mahavira, attempted to find Enlightenment through asceticism. The Jains developed the concept of ahimsa.

Jatakas—Birth tales. These stories tell of the lives Buddha lived before his reincarnation as Siddhartha Gautama.

Karma—Action and its response. The belief that any action, thought, or deed has a response that is positive or negative in terms of what it brings back to you, be it reward or demerit.

Lama—(Pali) A Tibetan teacher or master. Equivalent to Sanskrit guru.

Moksha—Ultimate release from the cycle of life, death, and rebirth. Reincarnation was a form of punishment, in a sense, because you weren't breaking this cycle.

Nirvana—(Sanskrit) Extinction or extinguishing; ultimate Enlightenment in the Buddhist tradition. PÇli: nibbÇna. Derivates: parinirvana (Sanskrit)/paranibbana (Pali)—Final liberation.

Pali—A language derived from Sanskrit in which much of the Buddhist literature is written; particularly, the Pali Canon—Buddha's discourses and teachings, which, previously, had only been known as an oral tradition.

Parinirvana—Physical death. It is the state of the end of a physical body, as well as when the spirit reaches nirvana.

Pratitya-samutpada—That the world is not made up of solids but is really a series of endless interlocking events

Reincarnation—The idea that a spirit, or an element of a soul, lives more than one life. Some people believe that an intact spirit lives many different lives, while Buddhists believe that there is no unchanging soul, so the soul is always altering throughout its many lives.

Samadhi—A state of focused meditation.

Samatha—Mental stabilization; tranquility meditation. Distinguished from vipÇssana meditation.

Samsara—The cycle of life, death, and rebirth. Buddhists want to release themselves from this cycle.

Sangha—The community of Buddhist monks and nuns, which also includes lay people.

Sanskrit—An ancient Indian language that is the language of Hinduism and the Vedas and that is the classical literary language of India. Many Buddhist words and terms are Sanskrit or derived from Sanskrit.

Sutra—(Pali) Scripture. Short aphoristic sayings and collections of those sayings. Sanskrit: sutta.

Three Poisons—The primary causes of unskillful action: Greed or selfishness, hatred or anger, ignorance, or delusion.

Tripitaka—The "Three Baskets" canon containing the sacred texts of Buddhism.

Vipassana—(Pali) Insight meditation that is part of a Buddhist practice. The other type of meditation is calm-abiding, or samatha. Sanskrit: vipaÊyana.

Yoga—Typically a system of postures (asanas) used by both Hindus and Buddhists to exercise the body as well as focus the mind.

REFERENCES AND RESOURCES

Books

Armstrong, Karen. *Buddha.* New York: Penguin Lives, 2001.

Auboyer, J., J.L. Nou, and H. Dumoulin. *Buddha: A Pictorial History of his Life and Legacy.* New York: Huston Smith Crossroad Publishing Company, 1983.

The Dalai Lama. *The World of Tibetan Buddhism.* Boston: Wisdom Publications, 1995.

Hesse, Herman. *Siddhartha.* Translated by Hilda Rosner New York: BantamBooks, 1951.

Keown, Damien. *Dictionary of Buddhism.* New York: Oxford University Press, 2003.

Maitreya, Ananda. *Trans. The Dhammapada.* Foreword by Thich Nhat Hanh. Berkeley, CA: Parallax Press, 1995.

Trainor, Kevin. Ed. *Buddhism: The Illustrated Guide.*, New York: Oxford University Press, 2004.

Magazines

Shambhala Sun at www.shambhalasun.com.

Tricycle: The Buddhist Review at www.tricycle.com.

Helpful Web sites

Buddhist Peace Fellowship: www.bpf.org

For World Religious Statistics: US State Department's International Religious Freedom Report 2004: www.adherents.com/Religions_By_Adherents.html

Online Sanskrit Dictionary:
www.alkhemy.com/sanskrit/dict/
www.belief.net

www.dalailama.com

www.jackkerouac.com

www.plumvillage.org

Acknowledgments

Once again, I owe a thank you to Holly Schmidt and Ken Fund for giving me the opportunity to write this book. I will always be grateful to them, too, for a wonderful three years at Rockport.

Thank you to Claire MacMaster, Ed Meagher, Rosalind Wanke, Elizabeth Muldowney, John Gettings, and Carol Holtz for their work on *The Buddha*. I would also like to thank John Poultney for his friendship and insight. My relationship with him was a significant step for me on my own path to Buddhism. It began when he asked me an important question "Can't you just *be*?" and told me that when I needed some peace of mind, I should sit outside and look at the ocean rather than try to get it from talking to people. How right he was! For these things, as well as for his affection, warmth, and support (and the laughter and the music…), I will always be grateful.

About the Author

Donna Raskin is a writer and yogo teacher who has practiced Buddhism for ten years. She has written for *Body + Soul, Cooking Light, Fit, Self, Shape, Woman's Day, Yoga Journal,* and is also the author of *Yoga Beats The Blues* (Fair Winds Press) and *The Single Woman's Guide to Real Estate* (Adams Media). You can read her column "Yogadonna's Guide to Life" in *FitYoga* magazine and visit her website, yogodonna.com. She lives with her son, James, in Rockport, Massachusetts.